Can celebrities change the
world?

At Issue

| Can Celebrities
| Change the World?

Other Books in the At Issue Series:

At Issue

Can Celebrities Change the World?

Roman Espejo, Book Editor

GREENHAVEN PRESS
A part of Gale, Cengage Learning

GALE
CENGAGE Learning™

Detroit • New York • San Francisco • New Haven, Conn • Waterville, Maine • London

12/08   # 227199384

GALE
CENGAGE Learning

Christine Nasso, *Publisher*
Elizabeth Des Chenes, *Managing Editor*

For more information, contact:
Greenhaven Press
27500 Drake Rd.
Farmington Hills, MI 48331-3535
Or you can visit our Internet site at gale.cengage.com

For product information and technology assistance, contact us at

Gale Customer Support, 1-800-877-4253
For permission to use material from this text or product, submit all requests online at
www.cengage.com/permissions

Further permissions questions can be emailed to permissionrequest@cengage.com

Articles in Greenhaven Press anthologies are often edited for length to meet page requirements. In addition, original titles of these works are changed to clearly present the main thesis and to explicitly indicate the author's opinion. Every effort is made to ensure that Greenhaven Press accurately reflects the original intent of the authors. Every effort has been made to trace the owners of copyrighted material.

Cover image © Images.com/Corbis

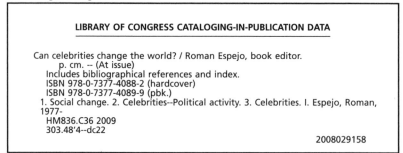

LIBRARY OF CONGRESS CATALOGING-IN-PUBLICATION DATA

Can celebrities change the world? / Roman Espejo, book editor.
p. cm. -- (At issue)
Includes bibliographical references and index.
ISBN 978-0-7377-4088-2 (hardcover)
ISBN 978-0-7377-4089-9 (pbk.)
1. Social change. 2. Celebrities--Political activity. 3. Celebrities. I. Espejo, Roman, 1977-
HM836.C36 2009
303.48'4--dc22
2008029158

Printed in the United States of America
1 2 3 4 5 6 7 12 11 10 09 08

Contents

Introduction

In May 2008, a lawyer representing Madonna announced the singer's plans to build a multimillion dollar school for underprivileged girls in Malawi, a small African country besieged by poverty, AIDS, and malaria. The school is the latest Malawian humanitarian project for Madonna; it follows her involvement in Raising Malawi, a children's organization she founded with Kabbalah Center co-director Michael Berg, and the release of *I Am Because We Are*, a 2008 documentary about the plight of Malawian orphans that Madonna financed, produced, and narrated.

Predictably, the plans of the "Queen of Pop" for the girls' school have not escaped scrutiny. Critics claim that the announcement is transparently contrived, as it was issued the day before Malawi's High Court had scheduled to make its final court ruling for Madonna and her husband's, British director Guy Ritchie, adoption of Malawian toddler David Banda. Dissenting this recent development, Canadian celebrity news Web site *Dose* offers this barb: "Though perhaps not the most subtle way to win over the Malawians before they decide her family's fate, no one can complain about Madonna's attempts to educate impoverished African girls (especially if the school institutes mandatory voguing lessons!)." On the contrary. David's father, Yohane Banda, stated to Reuters Television in the same month, "This is what I wanted, that Madonna should keep the child." (The High Court approved the adoption in late May.)

Madonna's multipronged Malawi mission is just one of numerous causes currently helmed by celebrities. Nonetheless, celebrity activism has been a facet of American culture for decades. In the 1930s, author Ernest Hemingway, celebrated for his sparse narrative style and known for his fascination with Spanish culture, championed the Loyalists in the Spanish civil war. In the 1970s, Academy Award–winning actress and political activist Jane Fonda, who achieved celebrity as a sex symbol, ignited controversy during the Vietnam War with several miscalculated, antiwar gestures (for which she was disparagingly nicknamed "Hanoi Jane"), and John Lennon's polarizing profile as a peace activist with radical ties all but eclipsed his fame as a member of the Beatles.

Numerous scholars and analysts, however, propose that today's culture is distinct from eras past in ways that cultivate a more powerful, further-reaching brand of celebrity influence. Darrell M. West, a political science professor and director of the Taubman Center for Public Policy at Brown University, alleges that, in an era marked by increasingly competitive media networks and rising political cynicism, the scales are tipping away from politicians, community leaders, religious figures, and researchers in favor of actors, recording artists, and athletes:

> While the contemporary era is not the first time celebrities have spoken out on questions of public policy, there are a number of factors in the current period that have given celebrities a far greater voice in civic affairs. The culture has changed in ways that glorify fame and fortune. The news industry has become highly competitive. Media reporters need good copy, and few sources provide better copy than actors, athletes, and entertainers. Voters are cynical and do not trust conventional politicians or experts. The fact that political advocacy has become very expensive places a premium on those such as celebrities who can attract attention and raise money.

In light of the historic Democratic presidential primaries of 2008, West's statements may have particular credence: When medial mogul Oprah Winfrey rallied with Democratic presidential candidate Barack Obama in Iowa in December 2007, it drew massive crowds and sent political analysts clambering to calculate Oprah's "O Factor" in their election forecasts. After all, Oprah's monthly book club and "Favorite Things" lists generate millions of dollars in sales and instant publicity.

Although some teenagers may be more in step with less politically engaged, more recently minted stars such as Zac Efron and Ashlee Simpson than pop culture totems such as Madonna and Oprah, the influence of celebrities on adolescents is an area of growing psychological, sociological, and cultural concern. Given the saturation of press on the mundane activities, transgressions, and judgment lapses of paparazzi-hounded celebrities such as Lindsay Lohan and Pete Doherty, youths—impressionable or not—are offered no-holds-barred, voyeuristic views of the stars they idolize.

To examine such potential influences, Susan Boon, a psychology professor at the University of Calgary, Canada, led a study on celebrities and teenagers. She concluded that adolescents often underestimate how much famous people influence them. According to Boon's findings, participants generally insist that celebrities do not inspire or shape their behavior, but more than half admit that they have been influenced or motivated by their favorite stars to engage in activities that range from productive to destructive, such as playing sports or smoking marijuana. Boon explains that "it's often hard to realize how much anyone influences us. We may also like to think that we develop our identity and sense of self rather than being influenced by others."

However, a survey of 12- to 18-year-olds carried out by *Weekly Reader* for the American Bible Society draws an opposing conclusion. Participants in the survey report that 67 percent of teens view their parents as role models, while only 16 percent identify celebrities as a primary influence. According to Sebra Roberts, a developmental psychology professor at Howard University, "There is a growing level of moral bankruptcy, a lack of spirituality in the media. No guidelines, everything goes." Therefore, Roberts maintains that when teen-

agers "see Britney Spears going crazy and stars dying young
. . . that is something they don't want for themselves."

Hollywood actors, chart-topping recording artists, and
record-breaking athletes will undoubtedly continue to align
themselves with social and political causes—to contribute to
society and use their fame and wealth for the greater good, to
retain the attention of the press and remain relevant, or, perhaps, for ambivalent motives that fall somewhere in between.
In *At Issue: Can Celebrities Change the World?*, journalists on
the celebrity beat to experts in the political arena offer their
viewpoints on whether star power, when used to spark social
change, enlightens or merely stupefies.

1

Celebrity Activism Can Be Influential

Leanne Shear

Leanne Shear is a New York City–based writer and author.

Celebrity activism is scrutinized for good reason: It frequently seems that celebrities adopt pet causes to maneuver themselves into the flattering light of strategic public relations. For instance, there are "training camps" they can enroll in to learn how to "get involved," while other A-listers are disingenuously hard-pressed to explain their involvement in their causes. However, for better or worse, the media centers itself on the famous and their activities to satiate the celebrity-obsessed public, in turn bringing much needed attention to social issues when household names partake in activism. Whether a celebrity's humanitarian or political interest is genuine or just for show, it is up to individuals to act upon the awareness the celebrity generates.

I couldn't believe it when my weeks of lobbying paid off and my editor at *Life & Style* magazine (where I freelance) finally gave me the go-ahead to hop on a train and head to Washington, D.C., on April 30, [2006] to cover the Save Darfur Coalition's rally against genocide in Darfur, Sudan.

But while this was to me a journalistic coup of epic proportions, it also offered up a twofold dilemma. First, it was clear my editor only agreed to send me to the rally because of its planned celebrity contingent: George Clooney and Russell Simmons would definitely be there.

Leanne Shear, "Celebrity Activists," *Wiretap*, May 31, 2006. www.wiretapmag.org. Reproduced by permission.

But in order to get any coverage of the event into the magazine at all, I needed to prod the various celebrity speakers and attendees into producing "newsworthy" (again, remembering that term is relative in the celebrity magazine context) quotes—without eclipsing or detracting from the utter seriousness of the purpose at hand. I was absolutely mortified at the prospect of asking the inane, stalker-ish questions so typical of the gossip magazines and quickly erased all thoughts of them from my head.

The second slice of my discomfort had to do with my inherent uncertainty about celebrities taking up humanitarian or political causes. As a rational human being, I know luminaries have brains like everyone else and are certainly capable of embracing a cause passionately. But my skepticism lingered over the issue of efficacy when the other 99 percent of their passion is splashed across "Page 6" or *In Touch*.

The current climate is obviously ripe for involvement. According to an article in the July 2, 2005, issue of *The Economist*, the business of aid in the 1990s "endured listless donors and woeful budgets. But now the mood and the money are on an upswing."

"Role Models"

Stars themselves have become a big part of this phenomenon—prolonged human suffering (including but not limited to famine, poverty and that wrought by natural disaster), it seems, is the sexy celebrity cause du jour. According to a 2005 article in *Time Europe* major issues like the internet, terrorism and the Iraq war don't necessarily "lend themselves to the high wattage celebrities can bring." Moreover, in a day and age of digitized and global media, it probably (hopefully?) becomes a lot harder for high-profile people to turn a blind eye to misery, especially for those who call themselves "role models."

There are even basic training camps for celebrities who want to get involved in something worthwhile but need a hand in understanding the issues. For example, the Creative Coalition brings together artists and celebrities to learn about causes, eventually enabling them to do things like lobby on their behalf in D.C. Similarly, Participate is a group linking up big films (and presumably their stars) with like-minded grass-roots organizations. Associations such as these, of course, do wonderful and important things. But the little devil perched on my shoulder is whispering that they also shroud the celebrities involved from the get-go with disingenuousness.

I arrived at the Darfur rally, then, with a secondary purpose: to try and determine what impact, if any, a celebrity could have on an important cause. I moseyed up to Nick Clooney (George wasn't doing any press at all) and asked him how he viewed the confluence of celebrity and humanitarian causes, especially considering the stature of his son. He told me, "We're in a culture of celebrity, and we all know it. It drives me crazy. But George [with his recent fact-finding mission to Chad and Darfur] said 'If you're going to take all these cameras and follow me, follow me here. Let's all find out something for ourselves that might be worthwhile for the whole human condition.'"

Similarly, Joey Cheek, (the Olympic speed skater who donated a total of $40,000 in prize money from his gold and silver medals to refugees in Darfur) told me, "For better or worse, at this point in our society, people look to celebrities. I think it's a bit of a travesty . . . but it's the reality we live in. If you have a brief moment of celebrity like I did at the Olympics, I thought it was better to do something useful, raise awareness."

In other words, they both know how to work the system, a fact that touches on something that as a gossip world "insider" never ceases to astound me: the collusion between celebrities, paparazzi, the gossip magazines and publicists/P.R.

There is absolutely nothing candid about these overlapping industries—in another article I wrote a few months ago, I called it the celebrity-industrial complex (only learning recently that I wasn't so brilliantly creative after all—it was actually *Vanity Fair* columnist Maureen Orth who first coined the term).

Quite simply, there's money to be made in all of these sectors, and that's why nobody or nothing is mitigating their proliferation, including the celebrities who "complain" about the intrusion of the paparazzi in their life. Where would they be without them? Certainly not on the cover of magazines, offering even more proof how loaded those relationships are from their inception.

[Celebrity activism] increases the awareness of people who otherwise simply might not have too firm a grasp on what's going on out there in the (increasingly complex) world.

Slate magazine editor Jacob Weisberg perfectly captures the spirit of the celebrity-industrial complex when he describes the surreal joint appearance of Condoleezza Rice, Hillary Clinton and Angelina Jolie September [2005] at a gala sponsored by the Global Business Coalition on HIV/AIDS. He depicts their photo op as a "state-of-the-art mélange of politics, celebrity and corporate public relations that such an event represents," adding, "cause-driven organizations want celebrity endorsements for the same reasons companies like Nike and Coca-Cola do. Whereas product endorsements pay cash, actors and musicians gain heft and responsibility by supporting fashionable crusades."

The True Litmus Test

And to a certain extent, that's fine. It's a phenomenon that increases the awareness of people who otherwise simply might not have too firm a grasp on what's going on out there in the (increasingly complex) world. But when does the trend stop and real knowledge and action take root? In other words, when will the average citizen who takes note of a celebrity endorsement actually absorb it into her consciousness and translate it into activity, even on the most micro of levels—perhaps the true litmus test of celebrity involvement in anything?

When I posed this question to Nick Clooney at the rally, he mused, "Well, that's up to each individual person, isn't it? All a celebrity can do is have the cameras follow them. Then it's our duty to either turn away—as many do—or follow that and do something about it." Similarly, Joey Cheek told me everyone needs to realize "there are as many problems as there are people to solve them. We are citizens of a global community," and it's time getting involved and making a positive impact on the world "became more than just celebrities or wealthy people."

I wasn't satisfied, and it became less difficult for me to see how the good deeds of Bono (crusader against AIDS and poverty in the third world) and his ilk have been met with more th   ttle critical skepticism. In a scathing op-ed in the *New*   *T*   author Paul Theroux (who spent many years   rica under the auspices of the Peace Corps) de-   sity (especially of celebrities, but specifically   houts "so loud people trust his answers")   le. the "more money platform" in Af-
1.   izing and a mistake, "donors en-
abl.   blind eye to bad governance,
rigge.   easons these countries are
failing.'   s home-grown citizen in-
volvemen.   tal brain drain—not the
computers .   ort Bill Gates wants to
send to places   e electricity, they don't
even have penci..

There is of course plenty of waste in the international aid business, and systemic corruption outside the African—and well into the western—paradigm. In *Kabul in Winter: Life Without Peace In Afghanistan*, [author] Ann Jones says matter-of-factly, "most of [international aid] goes to support the experts and contractors and bureaucrats of the donor[s] providing cover (and more tax dollars) for the rich in the guise of helping the poor."

So, OK, maybe Bono should have studied up a little harder on the intricacies of the international aid racket. However, it's infinitely worse—even critically damaging—when celebrity involvement in a humanitarian cause is merely a matter of self-promotion or a passing fancy. For example, I watched an interview with Lindsay Lohan recently on *Access Hollywood*. In it, she enthusiastically enumerated her upcoming movie projects, her love life, and scoffed off yet another round of those pesky party-animal rumors that seem to plague her. In practically the same breath, she told the reporter she's planning a trip to Kenya to contribute to the work of, of all things, the One campaign. It smacked of the superficial, feeling like little more than an attempt to be taken more seriously (perhaps bolstering the teen queen's quest for more "adult" movie roles?).

Or how about a few weeks ago, when I covered a charity event and had to interview a famous supermodel who was also the spokeswoman for the organization. She literally couldn't even answer the simple question "How did you get involved with the cause?" without some major prompting from the publicist/guard dog attached to her side.

Contrast all of that with an October [2005] CBS News/ Early Show "spotlight" about Angelina Jolie. She's been a goodwill ambassador for the U.N. refugee commission for over [seven] years and has been a central figure in a mind-boggling array of charities and geopolitical/humanitarian causes long before interest in her personal life reached its current fever pitch. In another interview, she said commitment is key to making a difference, noting, "We have to make sure we're willing to dedicate part of our lives to this. We shouldn't do it halfway."

Then there's Kanye West. He shocked the entire world when last year at a Red Cross event benefiting Hurricane Katrina victims, he looked right into the camera and said live on national television, enunciating each word, "George Bush doesn't care about black people." His outcry against the wrenching inequalities exposed by that disaster was raw, angry and emotional. But could anyone ever accuse him of being insincere? Hell, no.

Giving Rise to Awareness

Given all of the evidence, especially within the celebrity-industrial complex scenario, I suppose what each and every one of these celebrities—even the vapid or the stupid—do is, as previously pondered, give rise to some sort of awareness, which is (even when I am only grudgingly admitting it) in and of itself vital.

It's been my perception, maybe in large part given the genre of magazine in which I work, that too many American citizens, especially young Americans, have not been voting or paying attention to international politics. According to Generation Engage, a nonprofit devoted to urging young people to get more politically involved, people between the ages of 18 and 24 tend to vote in lower numbers than any other age group. But the group decries not a lack of young people's *interest* (they volunteer in community organizing and relief more than other age groups) but of their actual access to politicians and the process. That said, the 2004 presidential election brought out the largest percentage of young voters in 32 years, notching up 4 million new voters (at least half of which were Latino and black). What this seems to indicate is that when there is a reason to be passionate (ahem, George W.

Bush rancor), we young people will most certainly make our presence known. But the question remains: Does celebrity involvement make any real difference in what we choose to be passionate about?

If our readership of gossip magazines and consumption of celebrity culture is any indication, then the answer is yes. According to the Audit Bureau of Circulations, *In Touch, Us Weekly* and *Star* magazine had weekly circulation increases from 2005 to 2006 of 15.5 percent, 12.7 percent and 10 percent, respectively. However, the dominance of *People* magazine over all the other gossip weeklies, as a hybrid of straight gossip and stories with more of a human interest and humanitarian angle, leads me to believe there is more of a hunger in the general public for important, more serious articles than the editors at the rest of the gossip magazines so far have been willing to admit.

That's where the blogs come in, forcing the hand of the print magazines (across the board, most certainly not just in the celebrity sector) to become increasingly competitive in offering and breaking important news. According to blogcount, almost ⅓ of Americans regularly read blogs, and interestingly enough, while political blogs like Daily Kos (500,000 hits a day) and Talking Points Memo (150,000 hits a day) are increasing their readerships exponentially, especially among the young and internet-savvy, so are the more gossip-oriented blogs such as Gawker and Perez Hilton.

Maybe our skepticism [of celebrity activism] plays into the hands of "part of a larger conservative effort to delegitimize voices other than so-called 'authorities.'"

The popularity of these blogs suggests the confluence of celebrity and news in the same way that politicians are morphing into celebrities, and vice versa. Maybe we young people are inundated by the merger of the cause-driven and the celebrity-driven issues in our society and are frankly weary from trying to tease them apart. Maybe it doesn't, at the end of the day, matter to us whether a celebrity is invested in something important or something stupid, because the next hour, day or blog-post will bring another set of circumstances for us to ponder for ourselves.

As author Jeff Chang says, maybe our skepticism plays into the hands of "part of a larger conservative effort to delegitimize voices other than so-called 'authorities.'" In other words, "the conservative mind frame wants to limit the number of voices in a discourse." Kanye West might agree—our government and the corporations that pander to it could have a vested interest in keeping us dumbed down and focused on pure entertainment, immediately moving to discredit anyone—celebrity or not—who steps up to try and actually make a difference.

2

Celebrity Activism Is Limited

Douglas A. Hicks

Douglas A. Hicks is assistant professor of leadership studies and religion at the University of Richmond in Virginia and a Presbyterian minister.

Bono, lead singer of the world-famous Irish rock band U2, is a prime example of a celebrity activist. He spearheads several organizations, including the One Campaign, and works with the Live 8 concert series in attempts to increase awareness of—and end—poverty. Nonetheless, Bono is also lending credence to a lifestyle of material excess, which contradicts his humanitarian efforts. It is this lifestyle that is part of the economic problem of poverty, which the Irish rock star and his affiliate organizations fail to address. More importantly, the visibility of celebrities like Bono in the political arena reflects a regressing society that is shaped more by entertainers than political leaders.

In naming Bono Person of the Year, *Time* labeled him a good Samaritan. But this powerful biblical image misses the point of Bono's significance as a celebrity leader. He goes beyond being a high-profile good Samaritan—he stretches the moral imagination of his musical audience so that they, too, see the need to reach out to their global neighbors. In their own way, Bono and his band U2 deliver the message that we are, or at least can be, one world.

Bono has used his global celebrity to become an organizer and strategizer of Samaritans. He played a significant role in the Jubilee Campaign, which made unprecedented progress in gaining debt relief for highly indebted nations. He founded the organization DATA (Debt, AIDS, Trade, Africa) to work with governments and the international financial organizations to structure development assistance in effective ways. He has led the One Campaign, which seeks additional spending to alleviate global poverty, and worked with [Irish singer] Bob Geldof to arrange Live 8, the concurrent benefit concerts in all of the countries of the Group of Eight, or G8 (the world's eight largest economies). At the July 2005 G8 summit, the world's most powerful leaders committed to an additional $50 billion in annual debt relief. A number of those leaders met with Bono before and during the summit and have credited him with making this agreement happen.

It is these efforts in public education, communication and mobilization that make Bono's work an intriguing case of celebrity leadership. The One Campaign—like the Live 8 concerts—asks fans for no money but "only" a personal commitment to take a stand against poverty. During U2's sold-out concert tours, Bono declares nightly that the One Campaign, which already claims over 2 million members in the U.S., surpass the membership of the National Rifle Association [NRA] by 2008. [In March 2008, the One Campaign had 2.4 million members, the NRA about 4 million.]

Like that of the NRA, the One Campaign's goal is to communicate to leaders that there is a large bloc of citizens behind it—in this political case, citizens committed to addressing global poverty. Politicians, it is said, must be concerned in their public role not about citizens of other countries, however impoverished; rather, they must focus on the wants and needs of their own country's citizens. By making global poverty a concern of U.S. citizens, the One Campaign makes it a concern of U.S. Leaders. Even politicians who want to fight global poverty need this public pressure so they can claim that it is in their own interest to act. "Bono made me do it," they can say.

Not Able to Sustain the Momentum

Signing the pledge of the One Campaign requires very little. It is possible that Bono et al. will not be able to sustain the momentum to make a political difference. This is the point at which celebrity leadership can become a vice. At some point, the celebrity leader must motivate citizens to the point that they, in turn, motivate their political leaders.

It is a sign of the times that a celebrity is one of the most visible persons attacking global poverty. Where are our political and religious leaders?

This raises the question of how much motivation and how much commitment are needed to eradicate extreme poverty. In the grand scheme of things, the relative amount of money needed is small. The United Nations has asked industrialized countries to give 0.7 percent of their gross national product to fight poverty. This money, some $200 billion, would be far more than what is required to meet the basic human needs of the word's poor. The point: the level of commitment needed to address extreme poverty is not itself extreme. This stance is in sharp contrast to many past moral arguments, such as those of [Australian philosopher] Peter Singer, which imply that the affluent must make drastic lifestyle changes in order to meet the needs of the poor.

Some observers have asserted that a bigger change is needed. The affluence of the industrialized world, in which Bono is part of the wealthiest class, is a scandal to theological and moral understandings of global justice. In international terms, everyone reading this magazine is not just middle class, but rich. In Christian terms (or utilitarian, Aristotelian or Kantian terms, for that matter), we all have the resources with which to address extreme poverty.

This fact suggests another shortcoming of celebrity leadership. It takes for granted the culture of celebrity and affluence and overlooks the question of whether it is morally possible to live with integrity at any level of material comfort in our industrialized society.

Does staging a benefit, such as the Live 8 shows last summer, send not one but two lessons to concert goers? Although fans may learn to show concern about extreme poverty and sign up for the One Campaign, they may also receive the message that an economically privileged lifestyle, in which they buy CDs (promoted shamelessly by some of the performers) and enjoy expensive iPods, is morally acceptable. What if material excess is as harmful to us spiritually as absolute material poverty can be for the poor? Bono cannot lead that fight.

On this point, Bono would reply that his goal is actually more modest than a broad critique of Western affluence and entertainment. The sheer economics of the situation suggests that drastic improvement in the lives of the world's poor can be made by using resources that amount to little more than the crumbs on our tables. And, God knows, this would indeed be moral and theological progress.

It is a sign of the times that a celebrity is one of the most visible persons attacking global poverty. Where are our political and religious leaders? Why have they not already headed a more successful effort of their own? The answer is simply that even if we are not, in [the late cultural critic] Neil Postman's words, "amusing ourselves to death," our society is shaped more by entertainment than by politics and is more enamored with celebrities than moved by leaders.

Bono may well prove to be the most successful celebrity leader of our time. He is politically savvy and has used his visibility to leverage a movement that now has prominent international leaders talking about making poverty history.

When Celebrity Fades

But what happens when the celebrity fades? Bono's success hinges on the extent to which he can create an enduring institutional effort to reduce poverty—through organizations like DATA and the One Campaign and through lasting political changes in foreign-development assistance. The true measure of Bono's success as a leader is whether his movement can create and maintain an international structure that delivers political and economic change.

Can such an organized effort convince political leaders, not just once but over time, to act for debt relief and for human development in Africa and beyond? As Bono himself has acknowledged, the One Campaign and others like it should be considered successful if political leaders reshape their understanding of their own responsibilities. And in the end, holding political leaders accountable is the responsibility of citizens, not rock stars.

3

The Impacts of Celebrity Activism Are Mixed

Jonathan Curiel

Jonathan Curiel is a staff writer for the San Francisco Chronicle.

Celebrity activism is a phenomenon that has its benefits and drawbacks. Some famous activists, such as film star Angelina Jolie, are truly passionate about their causes and successfully have used their fame to direct attention to serious issues and spark change. Others, however, turn a blind eye to the corruption they may be supporting through fundraising, as is the case with star-backed events for ending poverty in Africa. And then there are the celebrities who jump on the bandwagon of fashionable causes in order to improve their public image and do not follow through on their commitments. However, in a society that is perpetually preoccupied with the famous, celebrity activism is a trend that's here to stay, whatever advantages and disadvantages it may bring.

The week was a typical one for actress Angelina Jolie. In the United States, she made the cover of every major magazine that traffics in celebrity gossip, all because of her romance with Brad Pitt. People ("Brad & Angelina Together in Morocco!"), Star ("Why Armed Guards Stormed Their Bedroom!") and the other tabloids spared no expense to get juicy details of Jolie's new affaire de coeur.

The movie star had little time to pay heed to the titillating headlines, nor was she likely to see them on newsstands in Si-

Jonathan Curiel, "Star Power: When Celebrities Support Causes, Who Winds Up Benefiting?" *San Francisco Chronicle*, June 5, 2005. www.sfgate.com. Reproduced by permission.

erra Leone, the impoverished African country where she spent the week of May 9 [2005] meeting Sierra Leone's [former] president and survivors of the country's 11-year civil war.

Jolie's confab with Ahmad Tejan Kabbah was historic, says one witness. Kabbah opened the meeting to civil rights groups in Sierra Leone (one of the few times he's ever done that), pledged to work with the organizations in the future and committed himself to responding to recommendations from the country's Truth and Reconciliation Commission.

Kabbah might not have taken any action were it not for the actress, says Gavin Simpson, a Sierra Leone activist who worked with Jolie during her visit to the West African country.

An example of star power? You bet.

The Perfect Humanitarian Advocate

On international issues, the tattooed, 30-year-old actress has greater clout than many U.N. diplomats with Ph.D.s. Jolie opens doors wherever she goes, whether it's a small country near the African equator or the capital of the United States, where Jolie has met some of Washington's top policy-makers to discuss refugee issues.

> *More stars than ever are pushing their political and social views into the public domain in an effort to change the world.*

"I see Angelina as the perfect humanitarian advocate," says Simpson, a member of the activist group Witness, in a phone interview from Sierra Leone. "She brings an immense amount of international focus and attention with her, but she never seeks to use it for her own benefit. On the contrary, she sends the spotlight directly to civic society advocates and makes them more effective and powerful in their own society."

Celebrities have always involved themselves in causes. Any list would have to include Audrey Hepburn, who worked with the United Nations International Children's Emergency Fund from 1988 until her death in 1993; [actor] Danny Kaye, who worked with UNICEF for 30 years, starting in the 1950s; and Humphrey Bogart, who led a 1947 group that protested the U.S. government's probe of communism in Hollywood. However, the last few years have seen a marked increase in the depth of their involvement.

Whether it's Bono flying to Africa with America's Treasury secretary, Sean Penn visiting Iraq to protest the then-impending war or Bruce Spingsteen stumping and strumming for [former presidential nominee] John Kerry, more stars than ever are pushing their political and social views into the public domain in an effort to change the world.

Whether this is a welcome development depends on your perspective. Organizations that work with the stars are ecstatic for the extra publicity they get. The week Jolie was in Sierra Leone, for example, she could have been promoting her new movie, *Mr. & Mrs. Smith*, which co-stars Pitt. . . .

Instead, Jolie chose to pay her own way to Sierra Leone so she could act as a representative for Witness, a New York organization started by musical celebrity Peter Gabriel that uses video technology to spotlight human rights causes.

Two Big Reasons

Why would anyone object to these efforts? Two big reasons: Suspicion of the celebrities' motives and a sense that the celebrities don't really understand the problems about which they speak.

Case in point: The lead singer for rock group Coldplay, Chris Martin, has visited Ghana in his campaign against Western trade practices that he says undermine farmers in the West African country. Get rid of unfair tariffs imposed on Ghana, and those farmers would thrive, he believes.

Martin, who's married to actress Gwyneth Paltrow, may be well-intentioned, but he's ignoring structural problems in Ghana that have far more impact than outside tariffs, says Franklin Cudjoe, a development director in Ghana's capital, Accra. Cudjoe derides what he calls rock-star economics—the practice of musician-activists and others to focus predominantly on the West's perceived responsibility for Africa's economic woes.

Cudjoe says "Live Aid" and other fund-raising efforts for the continent actually prop up corrupt governments in Africa. [In May 2005] "Live Aid" organizer Bob Geldof announced a new series of concerts, "Live 8," that will raise millions of dollars for Africa relief. The concerts will take place on July 2 [2005] in Philadelphia, Paris and other cities.

"Rock stars have been extending their social campaigns too far," Cudjoe says in a phone interview from Accra, where he directs the organization called Imani. "The more you keep giving aid to (African) countries, you are telling them, 'It's all right to run a bankrupt government.' The countries themselves have to be revitalized. But the governments themselves aren't interested in (changing). Chris Martin and Bono refuse to (acknowledge) that."

There are organizations that cater to celebrities who think they need help in understanding issues better and becoming better activists. These groups run workshops that teach them how to be effective speakers, introduce them to other activist-minded celebrities and suggest causes in which they can get involved.

The New York-based Creative Coalition (started in 1989 by Christopher Reeve, Susan Sarandon, Alec Baldwin, Ron Silver and others) specializes in arts-related issues, regularly sending its celebrity activists to lobby congressional leaders in Washington.

The interest is mutual. Recognizing the power of celebrities to draw media attention, Congress seeks out stars to testify at committee hearings and give the hearings more cachet. The practice can backfire, as in 1985, when then-Rep. Tom Daschle, D-S.D., had Jane Fonda and Jessica Lange—both of whom portrayed farmers in movies—testify during a committee hearing designed to protest President Reagan's proposed cuts in farm subsidies.

Political observers ridiculed Daschle for his emphasis on faux farmers, but 20 years later, celebrity activists are so commonplace that even global leaders regularly look to them for ideas.

[In January 2005], the World Economic Forum—that august body in Davos, Switzerland, that invites presidents and corporate heads to its annual retreat—had a special program featuring Jolie; Gabriel; Richard Gere; Sharon Stone; Lionel Richie, who was honored with an award for co-writing the 1985 fund-raising song, "We Are the World"; and Chris Tucker, the "Rush Hour" actor-comic who, in 2002, traveled with Secretary of State Colin Powell to a development summit in South Africa and with former President Bill Clinton on an AIDS fund-raising mission in Africa.

The Trend of Celebrity Advocacy

The stars were invited to analyze what the forum called this trend of celebrity advocacy. Skeptics were won over by the star panelists' answers and their commitment to their causes. It should be noted that some in the crowd rushed to take pictures of the panelists and to get their autographs.

People in the business of celebrity activism admit they've met the famous who tried to get involved with social causes but had no long-term interest in it.

"I was very impressed when I realized that these people were very serious," says Michel Ogrizek, a former medical doctor in Africa who, as the World Economic Forum's head of communications, was a panel participant. "When you are a celebrity, people think you are doing it just for PR and self-image. I'm what people call a cynical French (person), but I was fully convinced that these people were genuinely authentic."

Yet for every celebrity who gets invited to Davos, there are probably 10 who show no apparent desire to make the wider world a better place. People in the business of celebrity activism admit they've met the famous who tried to get involved with social causes but had no long-term interest in it, had no patience to learn about a subject they thought they'd wanted to embrace, and were not temperamentally suited to be more than a music star or movie star or whatever star they were.

Robin Bronk, the Creative Coalition's executive director, says, "Probably the most challenging thing one can do for one's career is get involved with an issue. It takes time. You put yourself out there, in that if you don't know why you're involved and what it is you're involved with and how to make a sensible argument, you're going to tank your own reputation."

If it's true that celebrity activism has become this trend, then Jolie and the rock singer Bono are two of today's leading trendsetters.

[In 2005] Bono established an "ethical" clothing line (Edun) that works with factories in Africa to promote fair trade. Since 1985, when his group, U2, became a musical giant, Bono has visited Africa many times to focus attention on AIDS, trade issues and other problems. At Davos and other forums, Bono, 45, often appears to know more about Africa's economies than specialists do.

"Celebrities open doors, without question—everyone wants to meet Bono—but the amazing thing about Bono is that they want to meet him again and again because he's not only a celebrity but knows far more about the subject under discussion than the politicians do," says Jeffrey Sachs, an economics professor at Columbia University who's worked with Bono for [nine] years.

Jolie has been a Goodwill Ambassador with the United Nations' High Commission on Refugees for [seven] years, traveling to the Sudan, Pakistan, Sierra Leone and other countries where refugee problems are a major concern. Jolie always pays her own way, and her work with the refugee commission is volunteer.

"Angelina Jolie pays every penny of her work with UN-HCR, and hazarding a guess, I'd say that might cost in the neighborhood of at least a couple hundred thousand dollars a year, minimum," says Shannon Boyd, who directs the refugee commission's Goodwill Ambassadors program. "It sets a new standard for the new generation of Goodwill Ambassadors."

Jolie has talked about her impetus for activism. "Just being an actress doesn't help me sleep well at night. When I do something for other people, then I feel my life has value."

In today's celebrity-obsessed culture, there may no better way to publicize a cause than having someone beautiful and famous show up and say, "This is important, and here is why."

Her fans who rush out this weekend to see "Mr. & Mrs. Smith" may not care about her activist work, but it's increasingly likely they're aware of it. The tabloids that follow Jolie and Pitt around the world have reported on her work in Africa and other continents and how Pitt has been moved to visit hospitals in Africa.

The Pitfalls and Potentials

Celebrity activism seems to be contagious, although the typical American may care more about Jolie's private life than her ability to meet with the president of Sierra Leone. The May 23

[2005] issue of *Us* magazine ran a five-paragraph story of Jolie's humanitarian work tucked inside a four-page cover story headlined, "How Angelina Stole Brad."

In today's celebrity-obsessed culture, there may no better way to publicize a cause than having someone beautiful and famous show up and say, "This is important, and here is why."

But the question remains: Why should it take an Angelina Jolie for people to care about the situation in Sierra Leone? For the U.N. refugee commission's Boyd, the answer is tied up in the reality of pop culture.

"Whether we like it or not, the popular culture is powerful, and not to recognize that is to have our head in the sand," Boyd says. "For refugees, we need to reach the mass public. Goodwill Ambassadors can go on prime-time TV shows that will never invite our senior-most friends, whether they're teaching at Harvard or sitting in the Senate. . . . A Goodwill Ambassador brings a special buzz if they are the right person, if they're well informed."

Boyd emphasizes the word "if"—a small word that nonetheless says a lot about the pitfalls and potential of celebrity activists.

4

Celebrity Activism Benefits International Affairs

Oscar Reyes

Oscar Reyes is a writer for Red Pepper, *a British political magazine.*

Cynics may find it easy to cast off celebrity activism in the world arena; it seems to wash away the groundwork laid by hardworking politicians and activists at no risk to the street-cred of participating celebrities. Nonetheless, celebrity activism is a lesson in cultural politics. From a public relations standpoint, star-backed endorsements can benefit a cause on an international level. For example, in 2004, best-selling author Arundhati Roy strategically used her fame to campaign against corporations profiting from Iraq and to give oppressed women in the region a chance to speak out. Moreover, celebrities activism reminds the public that they have the power to create the images of their political leaders as they do for their favorite stars.

[Irish singer] Bob Geldof calls one million demonstrators to Edinburgh. Round-the-world yachtswoman Dame Ellen MacArthur backs 'Sail 8', a flotilla of boats carrying G8 protesters. It can only be a matter of time before Tiger Woods joins the Peoples' Golf Association event at Gleneagles golf course.

Welcome to the era of celebrity-endorsed protest, where the hard work of grass-roots political organising can be swept aside at the whim of a few famous backers. It is tempting to

Oscar Reyes, "They Owe It All to Their Fans," *Red Pepper*, July 2005. www.redpepper .org.uk. Reproduced by permission.

sneer at the embrace of celebrity culture as a trivialisation of development issues, or worse, a patronising subversion of the real agenda by pin-headed pin-ups. After all, pop stars do their street-cred no harm by uniting around a feel good 'feed the world' message, but you're unlikely to see a Sugababes ballad about the WTO's [World Trade Organization] GATS (General Agreement on Trade in Services) any time soon. This argument has merits, but it ignores the more awkward fact that the celebrity succeeds in raising the profile of the very issues that campaigners are talking about.

The advent of Live 8 has achieved far more press coverage than months of Make Poverty History and Dissent! mobilisations combined. And with more than one million text messages scrambling for concert tickets, it has provoked the interest of the [animated mobile phone mascot] Crazy Frog generation way beyond the level that more conventional campaigns could hope to achieve. Organisers of protest trains to Edinburgh are still struggling to fill seats, and heretical whispers cam be heard on the activist grapevine: 'offer the trains to Geldof'.

For every charity record, there's a tour of Washington's Republican elite.

The Most Positive Lesson

The most positive lesson of this celebrity turn is that we should not ignore cultural politics. Successful protest movements have rarely brought people around to 'our' view. Rather, they have sought to engage with the feelings, norms and symbols of everyday life, and articulate them in a more progressive manner. Judged by this standard, the appearance of debt, aid and Africa on the agenda is an important political opening, since it poses questions about the eradication and causes of poverty to which the G8 is unlikely to find a convincing answer.

In opening one set of questions, however, celebrity endorsement closes others. This is the lesson of the original Band Aid and Live Aid in the 1980s. It was no mean feat to raise significant funds and, more importantly, raise the profile of African development in a context of Thatcherite indifference and me-first individualism. But those original interventions also cast Africans as victims of a process in which they had no agency of their own, no ability to question (let alone change) the conditions in which they found themselves. Geldof is still rehearsing the 'white man's burden' routine today, and the return of Live Aid brings with it the same negative stereotypes of Africa, the same failure to address the fact that between 1970 and 2002, Africa alone transferred $550bn to the North in debt repayments on loans estimated at $540bn, yet it continues to 'owe' some $300bn.

Celebrity-driven politics does not stop here, though. Where the 1980s campaigns focused on fundraising, today's 'politically conscious' stars front professionalised lobbying operations. For every impassioned plea to 'make me some f—ing money' (at least I think that's what Geldof said), there's a seat on the Africa Commission. And for every charity record, there's a tour of Washington's Republican elite.

U2's lead singer Bono is the acknowledged master of this political smooth-talking. He famously declared [former British Prime Minister] Blair and [current British prime minister Gordon] Brown to be the Lennon and McCartney of global development, and hailed former World Bank president James Wolfensohn as 'the Elvis of economics'. With less fanfare, he has also celebrated the role of the IMF, courted George Bush and far right Republican senator Jesse Helms, and could even be found sharing a joke with Geldof and [former] Russian president Vladimir Putin during the G8 summit in Genoa in 2001 as the city's streets burned. In 2002, Bono and Geldof launched DATA (Debt Aids Trade Africa), an awareness raising and lobbying group, which uses media attention to gain access to key decision-makers and unsurprisingly has the same agenda as the British government.

The "Great Men Theory"

Underlying this narrative is an old-fashioned 'great men theory': the idea that meaningful political change can be achieved by the few on behalf of the many. But what makes it work is something far more modern: the widespread penetration of government by public relations (PR).

Celebrities lobby politicians who, in turn, use campaigning techniques pioneered by celebrity publicists. This is not a wholly new phenomenon—as early as 1928, PR pioneer Edward Bernays brought a trainload of Broadway stars to the White House to project president Calvin Coolidge as having a 'warm, sympathetic personality'. But contemporary politics has taken this process further. Blair's willingness to be personally associated with 'eye catching initiatives', and his preference for softer, chat-show formats over hard-news interviews, are symptoms of a far wider process of focus groups, polls and surveys designed to maintain the right political image, using publicity techniques that extend deep into the policy-making process itself.

It can be argued that this is an appropriate form of politics for an information age. We need a clear point of reference to negotiate the complexity of our social interactions, so we place our trust in personality as a guide. But there are more immediate political concerns at work here, too. Ideological convergence around a market-driven politics means that today's politicians are no longer offering meaningful choices, different visions of how the world could be. And in this situation, personal reputation and image become increasingly important factors. Celebrity has stepped in because mainstream politics seems incapable of stirring our passions.

In the face of this, it would be tempting to turn our backs on celebrities altogether. But this approach doesn't always work. For example, when the World Social Forum (WSF) abolished plenaries—the platforms for major speakers—the same star system re-emerged anyway: with Venezuelan and Brazilian presidents [Hugo] Chavez and [Luiz Inácio Lula da Silva], in particular, playing court to political rallies far larger than the sessions that were scrapped. This is not simply a matter of bad faith. The politics of representation is alive and well, but it rests upon the recognition of faces above and beyond their formal authority. The WSF says that politicians can participate only in a personal capacity. But that personal capacity was shown to be a mobilising factor in itself, a source of legitimacy and popularity. Needless to say, the media circus followed suit—since its values system puts a premium on faces, on representatives who can articulate the demands of what it otherwise sees as a disordered mass.

In light of this, we should not reject celebrities but rather demand more from them. At the 2004 WSF in Mumbai, for example, novelist Arundhati Roy used her star status to call for a coordinated campaigning initiative against corporations profiting from Iraq. In other words, she sought to use her position to catalyse a common initiative, inviting us to 'bring our collective wisdom to bear on one single project' in a way that months of consensus meetings cannot. But at the same forum, she also gave a platform to *Dalit* women (oppressed by the caste system) to express their grievances. This is closer to what can be achieved: celebrity as catalyst, and celebrity as facilitator—not directly voicing the concerns of others, but giving up a platform for them to do so.

The Public's Gift

Politics in the extra-parliamentary mould could learn from this to mobilise a different kind of cultural politics. When politicians increasingly draw legitimacy from their personal profile, their trustworthiness, they become susceptible to attack on this same ground (as Blair did with the Iraq war).

What this teaches us, too, is that political power does not come to rest in the offices of government and multinational institutions. Public profile, image, trustworthiness: all of these are resources in the public's gift to bestow and to take away. Seen in these terms, power is better thought of as something dispersed, and that we are all capable of activating. This doesn't mean we ignore the traditional hubs of power, but instead understand them as places that gain legitimacy through our own belief in, or even identification with, the values of the personalities who inhabit and interact with them. It does mean we need to stop believing—a message that is hardly new to many activists. But the challenge remains to develop a cultural politics that can stir up political passions in the interests of a more democratic and radical form of political change.

5

Celebrity Activism May Not Benefit International Affairs

Daniel W. Drezner

Daniel W. Drezner is an associate professor of international politics at the Fletcher School at Tufts University. He is also author of All Politics Is Global.

Though celebrity activism is not new, the current wave of conscientious stars making headlines may not be making a significant impact on international affairs. In an age where fame can be achieved quickly and without merit, today's A-listers may engage in globe-spanning activism to differentiate themselves from their tabloid-fodder peers. More notable, however, is the shift in the media: Audiences increasingly obtain information on international affairs through "soft-news" programs that focus on celebrities, rather than "hard-news" sources such as newspapers and other news outlets. This gives public relations–savvy, but frequently unqualified, celebrities more media leverage than lesser-known, better informed experts, activists, and politicians. Finally, a spotty track record demonstrates that celebrity-endorsed foreign policy, though proven in bringing greater attention to and glamming up international affairs, does not establish a consensus about effectively solving international problems.

Who would you rather sit next to at your next Council on Foreign Relations roundtable: [Nobel Peace Prize winner and American politician] Henry Kissinger or Angelina Jolie? This is a question that citizens of the white-collared

Daniel W. Drezner, "Foreign Policy Goes Glam," *National Interest Online*, November 1, 2007. www.nationalinterest.org. Reproduced by permission.

foreign-policy establishment thought they'd never be asked. The massive attention paid to Paris Hilton's prison ordeal, Lindsay Lohan's shame spiral and anything Britney Spears has done, said or exposed has distracted pop-culture mavens from celebrities that were making nobler headlines.

Increasingly, celebrities are taking an active interest in world politics. When media maven Tina Brown attends a Council on Foreign Relations session, you know something fundamental has changed in the relationship between the world of celebrity and world politics. What's even stranger is that these efforts to glamorize foreign policy are actually affecting what governments do and say. The power of soft news has given star entertainers additional leverage to advance their causes. Their ability to raise issues to the top of the global agenda is growing. This does not mean that celebrities can solve the problems that bedevil the world. And not all celebrity activists are equal in their effectiveness. Nevertheless, politically-engaged stars cannot be dismissed as merely an amusing curiosity in foreign policy.

Consider the most notable example of a celebrity attempting to move the global agenda: Angelina Jolie. Her image has come a long way since her marriage to Billy Bob Thornton. In February of this year [2007] she published an op-ed in *The Washington Post* about the crisis in Darfur, referencing her work as a goodwill ambassador for the United Nations High Commissioner for Refugees. During the summer, her press junket to promote *A Mighty Heart* included interviews with *Foreign Policy's* website and a glowing profile in *Newsweek*, modestly titled "Angelina Jolie Wants to Save the World." In that story, former Secretary of State Colin Powell describes Jolie as "absolutely serious, absolutely informed. . . . She studies the issues." *Esquire's* July 2007 cover featured a sultry picture of Jolie—but the attached story suggested something even more provocative: "In post-9/11 America, Angelina Jolie is the best woman in the world *because* she is the most famous woman in the world—because she is not like you or me."

What in the name of Walter Scott's Personality Parade is going on? Why has international relations gone glam? Have stars like Jolie, Madonna, Bono, Sean Penn, Steven Spielberg, George Clooney and Sheryl Crow carved out a new way to become foreign-policy heavyweights? Policy *cognoscenti* might laugh off this question as absurd, but the career arc of Al Gore should give them pause. As a conventional politician, Gore made little headway in addressing the problem of global warming beyond negotiating a treaty that the United States never ratified. As a post-White House celebrity, Gore starred in *An Inconvenient Truth*, won an Oscar and a Nobel Peace Prize, promoted this past summer's Live Earth concert and re-framed the American debate about global warming. Gore has been far more successful as a celebrity activist than he ever was as vice president. This is the kind of parable that could lead aspiring policy wonks to wonder if the best way to command policy influence is to attend Julliard instead of the Fletcher School.

Joking aside, celebrity involvement in politics and policy is hardly new: Shirley Temple and Jane Fonda became known as much for their politics as their films. The template for Live Earth was the 1985 Live Aid concert, which in turn echoed the 1974 all-star concert for Bangladesh. Actors ranging from Ronald Reagan to Fred Thompson have taken the more traditional star route to power: running for political office.

[A] more selfish reason for celebrities to embrace policy activism: It distinguishes them from their tawdrier brethren.

Not everything old is new again, however. There is something different about the recent batch of celebrity activists. Current entertainers have greater incentives to adopt global causes than their precursors. Furthermore, they are more likely to be successful in pushing their policy agenda to the front of the queue. These facts have less to do with the celebrities themselves than with how citizens in the developed world consume information. Whether the rise of the celebrity activist will lead to policy improvements, however, is a more debatable proposition. Promoting a policy agenda is one thing; implementing it is another thing entirely. Regardless of what *Vanity Fair* or *Vogue* might want you to believe, celebrities really are just like everyone else. Some are competent in their activism, and some are . . . something else.

The Supply of Celebrity Activism

One reason for the newfound global agendas of celebrities is simply that today's stars have more autonomy than previous generations, and many of them recognize the benefits of being a popular saint. Stars may have always cared about politics, but they have not always been able to act on these impulses. Entertainers likely feared speaking out in the past, but the entertainment industry is not as authoritarian as it once was. The studio systems of yesteryear exerted much greater control over their movie stars. Mostly, the studios used this leverage to hush up scandals before the press found out about them. In the decades since, celebrities have acquired more leverage in Hollywood. In some cases—see Winfrey, Oprah—they have become moguls themselves. This gives them the autonomy to adopt pet causes, policy initiatives and make their own publicity missteps. It also affords them the opportunity to manage their own "brand", as it were. Just as Nike or Pepsi recognize the benefits of developing a positive brand image, so do George Clooney and Sheryl Crow.

This leads to another, somewhat more selfish reason for celebrities to embrace policy activism: It distinguishes them from their tawdrier brethren. We now live in a world where the path to fame can be as fast as a 15-second YouTube clip.

Paris Hilton became one of the world's most well-known faces on the strength of a famous name and a poorly lit home video. In such a world, marquee celebrities need to take steps to differentiate themselves from the lesser stars of stage and screen—or distance themselves from past scandals. So when Angelina Jolie attends the Davos Economic Forum or sponsors a Millennium Village in Cambodia, she's not only trying to do good, she's trying to create a brand image that lets Americans forget about her role in breaking up Brad Pitt and Jennifer Aniston.

The final reason more celebrities are interested in making the world a better place is that it is simply easier for anyone to become a policy activist today. An effective policy entrepreneur requires a few simple commodities: expertise, money and the ability to command the media's attention. Celebrities already have the latter two; the Internet has enabled them to catch up on information-gathering. Several celebrities even have "philanthropic advisors" to facilitate their activism. This does not mean that celebrities will become authentic experts on a country or issue. They can, however, acquire enough knowledge to pen an op-ed or sound competent on a talk show. And when they look sexy doing it, all bets are off.

The Power of Soft News

Even as star activists aspire to appear on hard-news outlets, they dominate soft-news programs—a different but no less influential media format. Celebrity activism matters more now because Americans get their information about the world in different ways from a generation ago. Way back in the twentieth century, the available news outlets were well-defined: the major television networks, the weekly news magazines, *The New York Times* and the local newspaper. By relying on the same "general interest intermediaries", the best and the brightest editorial gatekeepers forced most Americans to consume the same information. Clearly, the gates have been crashed.

Cable television, talk radio and weblogs have radically diversified the sources of news available to ordinary Americans. The market for news and entertainment has shifted from an oligopoly to a more competitive environment.

This shift in the information ecosystem profoundly affects how public opinion on foreign policy is formed. Matthew Baum has argued in *Soft News Goes to War* that a large share of Americans get their information about world politics from "soft-news" outlets like *Entertainment Tonight, Access Hollywood, SportsCenter, The View, Poeple, US Weekly, Vanity Fair, Vogue, The Daily Show, The Tonight Show,* or Gawker, TMZ and PerezHilton. Although viewers might not watch these shows or read these magazines to learn about the world, any reporting of current events aired on these programs reaches an audience unattainable to *The New York Times* or *Nightline*.

In the current media environment, a symbiotic relationship between celebrities and *cause célèbres* has developed. Celebrities have a comparative advantage over policy wonks because they have access to a wider array of media outlets, which translate into a wider audience of citizens. Superstars can go on *The Today Show* or *The Late Show* to plug their latest movie and their latest global cause. Because of their celebrity cachet, even hard-news programs will cover them—stories about celebrities can goose Nielsen ratings. With a few exceptions, like Barack Obama or John McCain, most politicians cannot make the reverse leap to soft-news outlets. Noncelebrity policy activists are virtually guaranteed to be shut out of these programs.

The growth of soft news gives celebrity activists enormous leverage. The famous and the fabulous are the bread and butter of entertainment programs. Covering celebrity do-gooders provides content that balances out, say, tabloid coverage of Nicole Richie's personal and legal troubles. ESPN can cover both Michael Vick's travails and Dikembe Mutombo's efforts to improve health care in sub-Saharan Africa. MTV will cover

Amy Winehouse's on-stage meltdowns, but they will also follow Angelina Jolie in her trips to Africa. They covered Live Earth for both the music *and* the message.

The power of soft news is not limited to television. *Vanity Fair* let Bono guest-edit a special issue about Africa, knowing that cover photos of Madonna and George Clooney would attract readers and buzz. Without intending to, those perusing the pages might form opinions about sending aid to sub-Saharan Africa in the process. Similarly, celebrity blogs can garner higher amounts of traffic. We may only speculate why Internet users flock to Pamela Anderson's website—but we know that while they are there, they can learn about Anderson's stance against animal testing.

Highlighting a problem is not the same thing as solving it, however—and the celebrity track record at affecting policy outcomes could best be characterized as mixed.

Indeed, celebrities actually have an advantage over other policy activists and experts because hard-news outlets have an incentive to cover them too. Celebrities mean greater attention, and hard-news outlets are not above stunts designed to attract readers or ratings. Consider this question: If *The Washington Post* is deciding between running an op-ed by Angelina Jolie and an op-ed by a lesser-known expert on Sudan, which author do you think they are most likely to choose?

Do Celebrity Do-Gooders Do Any Good?

There is no doubt that celebrities have the ability to raise the profile of issues near and dear to their hearts. Highlighting a problem is not the same thing as solving it, however—and the celebrity track record at affecting policy outcomes could best be characterized as mixed. Star activism has been reasonably successful at forcing powerful states to pledge action to assist the least-developed countries. It has been less successful at getting states to honor these pledges and not successful at all in affecting other global policy problems.

There have been some significant achievements, though. In the 1990s, Princess Diana embraced a ban on the use of land mines. Her death became a rallying point that led to Great Britain's ratification of the 1997 Ottawa Convention to ban the devices. The Jubilee 2000 campaign, which Bono championed, should also count as a success. According to the Center for Global Development, the movement to assist highly indebted poor countries resulted in "the most successful industrial-country movement aimed at combating world poverty for many years, perhaps in all recorded history." Celebrity activism also helped fuel the pledge at the 2005 Gleneagles G-8 summit to double aid to developing countries. Bob Geldof, who organized Live Aid a generation ago, arranged the Live 8 concerts to coincide with the summit. Bono, George Clooney, Claudia Schiffer and Nelson Mandela all appeared on stage.

To be clear, celebrities were not the only reason that the Ottawa Convention was signed or the G-7 launched the Highly Indebted Poor Countries initiative. In each of these cases, celebrities were buttressing organized, grassroots campaigns to change the status quo. At a minimum, however, star activists raised the media profile, spurring politicians to act sooner than they otherwise might have.

But there have been failures, too. While Bono provided an invaluable assist in promoting debt relief, he has not been as successful in his (Product) Red campaign. The idea was for consumers to do good through consumption—by buying iconic products colored red, a portion of the price would go to the UN Global Fund to Fight AIDS, Tuberculosis and Malaria. The campaign was launched in January 2006 to great fanfare at Davos. According to *Advertising Age*, however, it has been a bust: After an estimated $100 million in marketing expenditures, the campaign netted only $18 million. (Product)

Red has challenged the validity of these numbers, but the story invited media critiques of the campaign's strategy, denting its momentum and cachet.

Celebrity campaigns are also not always considered a greater good. Development expert William Easterly has argued that the celebrity focus on Africa's problems has been misguided. By focusing exclusively on the diseases of sub-Saharan Africa, celebrities have unwittingly tarnished an entire continent: "[Africans are] not helpless wards waiting for actors and rock stars to rescue them." Many African officials and activists share this sentiment, even heckling Bono at a development conference.

Though celebrities have a mixed record in promoting development aid to Africa, the record on other issues is even worse. The Live Earth concerts generated mixed reviews because of their disorganization. Promoters had to cancel the Istanbul venue because of a lack of local sponsorship, and the other concerts were less than sellouts. More significantly, some celebrity activists questioned whether the extravaganza even had a clear purpose. Bob Geldof told an interviewer, "Live Earth doesn't have a final goal. . . . So it's just an enormous pop concert or the umpteenth time that, say, Madonna or Coldplay get up on stage." Roger Daltrey of The Who concurred: "The last thing the planet needs is a rock concert."

Steven Spielberg came up for criticism in a *Wall Street Journal* article co-authored by actress Mia Farrow. The article warned that Spielberg, as an "artistic advisor" to the 2008 Summer Olympic in China, would become "the Leni Riefenstahl of the Beijing Games" if he did not speak out. The chastised producer later sent a letter to Chinese Premier Hu Jintao because he felt compelled to "add my voice to those who ask that China change its policy towards Sudan." Regardless of the reasons, Beijing has begun to pressure Sudan's government into cooperating with the United Nations on Darfur.

Richard Gere has devoted decades to the cause of Tibetan independence to little avail. Yet with one onstage kiss of Bollywood star Shilpa Shetty, he did manage to get himself burned in effigy across India—the reverse celebrity problem. On the whole, celebrities have made little headway in bringing peace to all the world's trouble spots.

Even if celebrities are judicious and focused in promoting their causes, there are diminishing marginal returns to activism. A celebrity who repeatedly harps on a particular cause risks generating compassion fatigue with the general public. As Bono recently told CNN, "Look, I'm Bono and I'm sick of Bono. And I fully understand. . . . I look forward to a time when I'm not such a pest and a self-righteous rock-star. Who needs one?" Clearly, there is a fine line to walk between sustained focus and righteous indignation.

Hindered Hollywood

It is true that star activism can influence the global policy agenda. But as we've seen, when it comes to concrete achievements, celebrities have a spotty track record. They face a number of constraints on their ability to affect policy. Most obviously, celebrities might not be the most grounded community of individuals. While some celebrities have mastered the activist game, others seem out of their depth. Hip-hop singer and Live Earth performer Akon admitted to reporters that he didn't know what it meant to be "green" until the day of the concert. Sean Penn's recent fact-finding trip to visit Venezuelan president Hugo Chávez served little purpose beyond a story in *The New York Times* that gently mocked both men. Then there's Peter Gabriel's idea for "The Elders", a group which includes Nobel Laureates Jimmy Carter, Nelson Mandela and Desmond Tutu that tries to "use their unique collective skills to catalyze peaceful resolutions to long-standing conflicts"—something that seems more at home in a *Matrix* sequel than in the here and now. For every Bono or Angelina Jolie, there are other celebrities who are less well-versed in their cause *du jour*. The problem for the savvy stars is that when other entertainers act foolishly, it becomes easier to summarily dismiss all celebrity activism.

Another problem is that some celebrity causes are more controversial than others—and controversy can still threaten a star's bankability. Tom Cruise's sofa pitch for Scientology (and against psychiatry) likely played a role in Paramount's 2006 decision to sever its business relationship with him. When the Dixie Chicks blasted George W. Bush on stage at a 2004 London concert, radio stations pulled their chart-topping single from playlists, affecting the record's sales.

It is therefore not surprising that celebs have had their greatest successes in touting humanitarian causes and almost no effect on ending militarized conflicts.

None of these episodes ended a career, but they did sting. These cautionary tales reveal a clear constraint on celebrity activism: Most stars will be reluctant to risk their professional careers to take a controversial political stance. When Michael Jordan was asked to endorse a Democratic senatorial candidate during his playing career, he demurred with a famous reply: "Republicans buy sneakers too." There are certainly those who present exceptions to this rule, such as Robert Redford, Michael Moore and Susan Sarandon—but they are not the rule.

A deeper problem celebrities face is that the implicit theory of politics that guides their activism does not necessarily apply to all facets of international relations. The goal of most social activism is to bring greater attention to a problem. The assumption is that once people become aware of the problem, there will be a groundswell of support for direct action. This is not how politics necessarily works, particularly in the global realm. Any solution to a problem like global warming, for example, involves significant costs. As people become more aware of the policy problem, it is far from guaranteed that a consensus will emerge about the best way to solve it. It is therefore not surprising that celebs have had their greatest successes in touting humanitarian causes and almost no effect on ending militarized conflicts.

Principled Activism and Righteous Indignation

This increase in influence comes with a warning, however: With great power comes the great potential for blowback. A September CBS/*New York Times* poll revealed that 49 percent of Americans think celebrities should stay out of politics. Since 2003, the polling data suggests increasing public hostility towards celebrity activism.

Both elites and ordinary citizens have their reasons to resent star power. Celebrity activism rubs many policymakers and pundits the wrong way. To some, star power upsets their sense of fair play. Christopher Caldwell complained recently, "Philanthropy is a route through which celebrity can be laundered into political power." He makes an interesting point. Why should the leads of *Mr. & Mrs. Smith* be listened to on weightier affairs of state? Who appointed Bono the global secretary of development? Does Pamela Anderson merit attention for her causes ahead of learned policy experts? To other aspirants of the foreign-policy community, the offense is more personal. Power is a zero-sum commodity, and if celebrities are rising in influence, that means others are falling. This will not sit well with those who feel pushed aside, especially if they have toiled for years in graduate school and low-paying policy jobs.

Among "ordinary" citizens, celebrities are all too aware that the ingredients for a fall from grace are interwoven with the sources of star power. At its core, star activism hints that the famous are somehow better than you or me. Some Americans view celebrities who pontificate on politics and policy as taking advantage of a bully pulpit that they did not earn. There's a fine line between principled activism and righteous indignation, and the celebrity who crosses that line risks incurring the wrath of the common man or woman. Americans are addicted to celebrities because we like to see them on top—but we also enjoy their fall.

6

Celebrity Activism May Benefit Africa

Madeleine Bunting

Madeleine Bunting is associate editor and a columnist at the British newspaper the Guardian.

Live 8, the series of benefit concerts held in 2005 intended to raise awareness of poverty in Africa and other nations, are important. The massive marketing, advertising, and public relation campaigns used in Live 8 demonstrate that a small group of people—globally famous celebrities, in this case—have given momentum to the African agenda. These star-studded events may dwarf grassroots-level movements in the eyes of the media, but "traditional" activism itself has a track record of diminished returns. Other issues, such as the lack of African voices and the patronizing of impoverished countries by wealthy northern nations, do have weight. But in a short-attention-span, consumerist world, Africa may need events like Live 8 to remain in the headlines.

Ever heard of the Millennium Development Goals? Could you name two of them? Do a spot check in your nearest McDonald's and chances are you'll draw nothing but bewilderment. So before the cynics and sceptics pounce on [British screenwriter] Richard Curtis's The Girl in the Cafe on BBC 1 this Saturday, it's worth pointing out that it will reach a prime-time audience in a way that decades of campaigning have failed to do. The love story of a socially illiterate civil servant and an ex-convict at a G8 summit may provide a clunky vehicle for some old-fashioned agitprop but, hey, at least you get a chance to explain the goals to millions (and Curtis makes sure it's at indecently generous length).

For Make Poverty History, it's one more coup after a series of front-page stories ranging from a G8 landmark deal on Africa to [Irish singer] Bob Geldof's dotty appetite for drama with calls for a Dunkirk flotilla and a million people marching on Edinburgh. Africa is on the national agenda in a way it has never been before—the focus is far broader than a particular emergency such as a famine. The development activists who have doggedly spent years organising meetings in smelly student union halls and stuffing envelopes may be slightly bewildered by the erratic commandeering of their cause by a group of well-connected celebrities, but they are not complaining.

No complaints even that the Make Poverty History rally in Edinburgh on July 2 [2005]—in the planning for months—will be dwarfed by Live 8 on the same day (an event that Geldof only agreed to put on at the very last minute, despite a year of pleading). The timing couldn't be worse and, to top it, Geldof has launched his own rally on July 6. But again, no one is complaining.

The point isn't that there are some grave concerns about the style and content of this campaign, but that no one is voicing them before they've seen whether it works. The depressingly small returns for traditional campaigning—the postcards, the lobbying—have led to a sense of quiet desperation among aid agencies. The kind of change in policy they want is so dramatic that they have had to find new ways to mobilise mass support. That was exactly the conclusion of a small group of well-connected celebrities—Bono, Geldof and Richard Curtis, writer of Notting Hill and one of the founders of Comic Relief.

The result is a new experiment in campaigning. It has drawn much more heavily on the expertise of marketing, advertising and PR to shape—not just push—its message and generate momentum, and that's evident in three ways. First, they've framed the campaign as a unique, time-limited offer: a once-in-a-generation chance. It's the technique used to sell limited editions of exclusive handbags: buy now while stocks last!

Second, the adman is all over the product; it's got to offer the feel-good factor. A bit glam, some show business, lots of product placement (white bands on celebrity wrists), lots of product endorsement (Bono's pitch on his Vertigo tour, Brad Pitt's primetime television). The borders between consumerism and protest—already blurred by the likes of the Body Shop—are disappearing fast, and now you can do both at the same time. Forget the sore feet, bursting bladder and the hard-to-hear speeches of an old-fashioned rally, this time you can picnic in the park with a beer at Live 8 and still feel good.

Third, make it simple and stay on message: a baby dies every three seconds; the eight men meeting in Gleneagles can do something about it. It is the first time that a cause has been mass-marketed with this kind of coordination across the developed world and with this kind of saturation impact.

Capturing the Political Agenda

Kirsty Milne, in Manufacturing Dissent (her recent analysis of single-issue politics in the UK), pointed to "dramatic surges of single-issue sentiment that occur outside party politics and that can be activated by a surprisingly small group of people". She was writing about the fuel protesters and the Countryside Alliance, but Make Poverty History has used the same tactics of putting together a "short-lived coalition that can capture the political agenda". Milne's central argument was that "protest had migrated from the street to the newspaper"—in the case of Make Poverty History, it has migrated to the celebrity dinner party.

What is an extraordinary phenomenon is the access of celebrities such as Bono and Geldof to almost everyone—presidents, prime ministers, film and rock stars, newspaper editors, television executives, bankers and billionaires. Bono's lobbying in the US, UK and Europe shows how a political and corporate world is hungrily casting round for new sources of legitimacy to bolster its positions—and how celebrities can use that vulnerability to advance their cause.

The drawbacks to this model of campaigning are obvious: there has been no attempt to manage expectations—when they fail to make poverty history on December 31, 2005 (as they will), what happens? How will they answer the charge that if it was "a once-in-a-generation chance", there's no point campaigning again for 20-odd years? What haunts me is the weary scepticism that will greet any suggestion of Africa in 2006. Done that, been there, got the T-shirt.

The strategy is bold but risky—it's blowing the expense account; Africa won't get public attention like this again for a long time, yet Africa needs a generation (at least) of sustained campaigning if it is to have any chance of tackling the catastrophe of Aids and its particular vulnerability to the looming crisis of climate change. Plus, there's the increasingly embarrassing problem that African voices are virtually non-existent—not just their bizarre omission from Live 8, but everywhere; this is the rich north talking to itself about another continent's future. That is mighty lopsided.

Finally, the message has been simplified to fit a storyline, rather than describe reality. The G8 is the forum where rhetoric and aspirations are pronounced; the work doesn't end when they leave Gleneagles, it starts. We've had G8s with historic announcements on Africa before (e.g., Lyons in 1996), but without relentless pressure, nothing much materialises. Solving world poverty is not half as easy as some of the campaign rhetoric implies.

But I'm prepared to be convinced that these drawbacks are a price worth paying to make a big hit or a "flash moment", in the phrase cited by Milne. The impatience of consumer culture with the complex and the slow moving might mean that certain marketing tricks are necessary to capture short attention spans. As Milne points out: "For a generation that can vote someone out of the Big Brother house in minutes, a month-long media uproar makes more sense."

"Media uproar" gives the illusion of a lot of support—are those watching Live 8 protesting or enjoying themselves?—and politicians are responsive to that. It doesn't fit the template of how we have understood politics and protest in the past, but I'm hoping that doesn't mean it won't work.

7

Celebrity Activism Does Not Benefit Africa

Stuart Hodkinson

Stuart Hodkinson is a writer for Red Pepper, *a British-based political magazine.*

The series of benefit concerts in 2005, Live 8, that were intended to put an end to poverty in Africa and other impoverished places, failed. The figures of aid for Africa touted by its famous organizers were wholly exaggerated. Also, the debt relief plan, which promised to cancel 100 percent of the debts of fourteen African and four other nations, was not followed through. More outrageous, besides the posing and collaboration of Live 8 celebrities in what were actually lies, was the paternalistic, pitying attitude of Live 8. It gave neither African activists nor artists platforms to speak. The spin-doctored success of such superficial, celebrity-powered bids to end poverty undermines the work, progress, and problem-solving demands made by grassroots organizations like Make Poverty History, whose 200,000-strong protest in Edinburgh in 2005 did not stand a chance against free star-studded pop concerts.

Remember Make Poverty History [MPH], anyone? It seems a long time ago that some 200,000 people flocked to Edinburgh on 2 July [2005] to rally G8 leaders as part of an unprecedented global justice campaign. That same day, [Irish singer] Bob Geldof organised free music concerts in nine countries worldwide under the Live 8 banner. The demands

Stuart Hodkinson, "G8—Africa Nil," *Red Pepper*, November, 2005. www.redpepper.org.uk. Reproduced by permission.

were straightforward and reasonable: rich countries should boost overseas aid in line with 35-year-old unmet promises; cancel completely the debts of the 62 poorest countries; set binding dates for the abolition of subsidies and other protectionist support to Northern farmers; and stop forcing liberalisation and privatisation on poor countries, whether in international trade negotiations or as conditions of aid and debt deals.

Six days later, in the shadow of the 7 July bombs that ripped through central London, the Gleneagles summit ended to a chorus of rock star cheers. 'This has been the most important summit there ever has been for Africa,' Bob Geldof confidently stated at the post-summit press conference. 'There are no equivocations. Africa and the poor of that continent have got more from the last three days than they have ever got at any previous summit . . . On aid, ten out of ten. On debt, eight out of ten. On trade . . . it is quite clear that this summit, uniquely, decided that enforced liberalisation must no longer take place,' he said, before finishing with a flourish. 'That is a serious, excellent result on trade.' Bono, voice cracking with emotion concurred: 'We are talking about $25 billion of new money . . . The world spoke and the politicians listened.'

Mission Accomplished

Assembled journalists and campaigners broke into spontaneous applause; the next day's media coverage led with Geldof's 'mission accomplished' verdict. But as the millions who signed up to Make Poverty History and Live 8 no doubt rejoiced, inside the upper echelons of MPH all hell was breaking loose. 'They've shared us,' a press officer from a UK development NGO [non-governmental organization] screamed down the phone. Indeed they had. Moments earlier, Kumi Naidoo, the veteran South African anti-apartheid campaigner and current chair of MPH's international umbrella, the Global Call to Action against Poverty (G-CAP), had delivered the coalition's official response: 'The people have roared but the G8 has whispered. The promise to deliver [more aid] by 2010 is like waiting five years before responding to the tsunami.'

Having pored over leaked drafts of the G8 communiqué into the early hours, MPH officials knew that the G8's announcements on aid, trade and debt were not only grossly inadequate to help poor countries reach the UN's millennium development goals by 2015. They were also completely bogus—and they had briefed the rock stars to that effect. More than half of the promised $50 billion in aid—which wouldn't kick in until 2010—wasn't really new money at all, but a dishonest amalgam of old pledges, future aid budgets and debt relief. And despite agreeing that 'poor countries should be free to determine their own economic policies', only Britain had announced it would no longer tie overseas aid to free market reforms—a promise it would instantly break in the G8 debt deal. The US, in contrast, had made it immediately clear at Gleneagles that aid increases would require 'reciprocal liberalisation' by developing countries. Worse, as Yifat Susskind, associate director of the US-based women's human rights organisation, Madre, explains, Bush's 'millennium challenge account', specifically praised by Bono and Geldof, 'explicitly ties aid to cooperation in the US's "war on terror"'.

The much lauded June G7 (G8 minus Russia) finance ministers' '$55 billion' debt deal, in which 18 countries—14 of them African—would receive '100 per cent multilateral debt cancellation', with 20 more countries soon to follow, was a similar pop star-veiled deception. In reality, the G7 had only agreed to take over the debt repayments of those countries to just three of world's 19 multilateral creditors—the IMF, World Bank and the African Development Bank (ADB)—meaning they would continue to be saddled with crippling debts owed to the other 16.

What's more, the $55 billion figure would in reality be worth little more than $1 billion a year—the amount paid out in annual interest payments to the World Bank, IMF and ADB by the 18 countries as a whole. To put this in context, African countries alone have a staggering $295 billion official debt stock, having already paid back $550 billion in interest on a total of $540 billion in loans between 1970 and 2002. In 2003, developing countries paid out a crippling $23.6 billion in debt servicing.

Despite the G8's promise that debt relief would be 'unconditional', the 18 countries selected had just completed nine years of neoliberal structural adjustment under the IMF/ World Bank's Heavily Indebted Poor Country (HIPC) scheme, which has typically increased poverty and inequality at the same time as privatising and liberalising large swathes of their economies. The 20 countries additionally earmarked for debt cancellation must now also submit to the HIPC process. Incredibly, for every dollar received in debt relief, poor countries will receive an equivalent dollar reduction in aid.

People must not be fooled by the celebrities: Africa got nothing.

A Complete Lie

As Eric Toussaint, of the Belgium-based Committee for the Abolition of the Third World Debt (CADTM), argues: 'This precious funding will only be returned if countries meet "specific policy criteria"—more long years of privatisation and liberalisation that increases school fees, health-care costs and VAT [Value-added-tax], removes subsidies for basic products and creates unfair competition between local producers and transnational corporations, all of which hurts the poor. For Geldof to stand there and say that conditionality is over was a complete lie.'

The same is true of trade. Contrary to Geldof, the G8 did not decide that from now on rich countries would no longer force through neoliberal trade policies in developing countries ahead of 6 December's World Trade Organisation ministerial meeting in Hong Kong. According to Martin Khor, of Third World Network, the influential international research and advocacy body based in Malaysia: 'The G8 summit did not indicate any change of heart from the aggressive campaign their negotiators are pursuing in talks to rapidly open up the developing countries' agricultural, industrial and services sectors.'

All in all, despite nearly a year of intense lobbying and campaigning for G8 countries to change course in order to meet the UN's millenium development goals, Gleneagles, in the words of Christian Aid's Claire Melamed, was a 'grave disappointment'. Senegalese economist Demba Moussa Dembele, of the African Forum on Alternatives, puts it more forcefully: 'People must not be fooled by the celebrities: Africa got nothing.'

Given this assessment, Geldof and Bono's misrepresentation of the G8 deal at the post-summit press conference came as a severe blow to many within MPH. Helped by four British Muslim suicide bombers in London, the rock stars ensured that the issues of Africa, poverty and development disappeared from the media spotlight within days of the summit's end. Four months on [in November 2005], and despite the disaster of the G8 for worldwide efforts to eradicate poverty, the silence of MPH is deafening.

Contrary to appearances, however, the coalition has not disbanded. In fact, it has decided to carry on as a campaigning movement after the Hong Kong WTO ministerial meeting in December. Inside the coalition, moreover, there is anything but silence. In the depressing aftermath of Gleneagles, the political disagreements that gripped MPH during the spring and summer months between the powerful grouping of government-friendly aid agencies and charities effectively running MPH, led by Oxfam and including CAFOD [Catholic Agency for Overseas Development], Save the Children Fund and Comic Relief, and the more progressive yet smaller NGOs like War on Want and the World Development Movement, have escalated. But this time, the unhappiness at how MPH has been manoeuvred so closely to New Labour by leading charities and celebrities stretches way beyond the coalition's radical fringe.

Too Superficial

'The campaign has been too superficial,' argues Christian Aid's head of policy, Charles Abugre. 'Numbers have been more important than politics and we have placed too much emphasis on celebrities with strong connections to those in power. Consequently, a serious occasion was turned into a celebration of celebrities.'

There were millions of people watching the concerts, but what was the analysis? What was the message?

In July [2005] Red Pepper reported how critical policy positions and stances agreed [to] within the coalition were being lost in the 'public messaging' thanks to the efforts of Oxfam and film-maker Richard Curtis. Instead of criticising Blair and Brown, MPH spin doctors and their cast of celebrities were going out of their way to praise them. The news that MPH was organising a massive demonstration in Edinburgh on the eve of the G8 was quickly corrected by MPH spin doctors as a 'walk ... to welcome the G8 leaders to Scotland ... The emphasis is on fun in the sun.'

Since then, Red Pepper has learned that right up until the early hours of 8 July, members of MPH's coordinating team were having to face down a desperate last-ditch effort from within to secure a positive civil society reaction to the G8 communiqué. According to one insider, this came after weeks of internal pressure on some NGOs to 'clear delicate stories with the Treasury', and attempts by Justin Forsyth, Oxfam's former policy chief turned Downing St special advisor, to pressure leading NGO officials 'to refrain from criticising the government' as it became increasingly obvious that the Gleneagles outcome would not be 'historic'. Following Forsyth's anger at Kumi Naidoo's negative assessment of the G8 at the post-summit press conference, the pair had to be 'physically separated' backstage.

The debate is most intense over the organisation of Live 8, which to many has come to symbolise the damaging behaviour of Geldof, Bono and [British screen writer] Richard Curtis. 'There were millions of people watching the concerts, but what was the analysis? What was the message?' asks Charles Abugre, who believes Make Poverty History's methodology set the tone for the Live 8 whitewash. 'It was one of handouts and charity, not one of liberation defined by Africans themselves or the reality that we are actually resisting neo-colonialism and neoliberalism ourselves.'

[A] hastily arranged, low-key Live 8 concert in Cornwall featuring African artists ... was attended by just 5,000 people.

While much has been written in the mainstream press about how Live 8 came to happen, there has been little coverage of how bitterly most MPH members still feel about the concerts, which were secretly organised behind their backs by Geldof and Curtis with the full knowledge of Oxfam, Comic Relief and the Treasury. This is not just because they completely overshadowed MPH's own rally in Edinburgh on 2 July. Campaigners feel that Live 8 and Geldof hijacked the MPH campaign for a very different cause. Their focus was not on global poverty, but Africa. And their demands were not those of MPH, but of the Commission for Africa, a government-sponsored think-tank whose members, hand-picked by Blair and Brown, were described by Professor Paul Cammack, writing in these pages, as a 'web of bankers, industrialists and political leaders with connections to the IMF and the World Bank, all committed to spreading the gospel of free market capitalism'.

Paternalistic Treatment

The coalition's anger at the Live 8 organisers has intensified over revelations about their paternalistic treatment of African campaigners and their relationship to corporations operating in Africa. Firoze Manji, the co-director of Fahamu, an African social justice network and member of G-CAP, recounts how the African coalition had already planned a concert in Johannesburg in early July to be held in one of the townships to encourage maximum participation of the people who suffer the greatest effects of globalisation and neoliberal policies. However, according to Manji, a private meeting in London of Oxfam GB, Curtis, Geldof and Kumi Naidoo, G-CAP chair and director of Civicus, the South African-based global alliance for citizen participation, unilaterally cancelled the original concert in favour of the Live 8 event, throwing the African coalition into disarray. The concert, which cost some $500,000 to stage, was attended by just 4,000 people.

Back in Britain, having excluded African artists from the main London concert, saying Live 8 was 'not a cultural event' and only musicians with more than four million record sales could play, lest people would 'switch off', Geldof eventually gave his blessing to 'Africa Calling'. This was a hastily arranged, low-key Live 8 concert in Cornwall featuring African artists that was attended by just 5,000 people. Scandalously, the corporate sponsors assembled by the organisers included: Nestlé, accused of exploiting the HIV/Aids epidemic in Africa to sell more milk substitute products to infected mothers; Rio Tinto, the world's largest mining corporation, widely condemned for its longstanding record of human rights and environmental abuses across the global South; and Britain's biggest arms manufacturer, BAE Systems, whose export-led agenda, according Mike Lewis of the UK's Campaign Against Arms Trade (CAAT), is 'fuelling conflicts across Africa, with catastrophic impacts on development, and diverting spending away from health and education'.

There is now growing pressure coming from inside the coalition to distance itself from the celebrity set. This has particularly angered Oxfam, and insiders believe that the aid agency will now lead a break away split from MPH, taking Comic Relief and Bono's charity, Debt, Aids, Trade, Africa (DATA), with it. Given Oxfam's avowedly free trade solutions to third world poverty, and, along with Comic Relief's Richard Curtis, Bono and Geldof, its leadership's uncomfortably close relationship to New Labour, this scenario could be an encouraging development for efforts to realign MPH in the direction of the global justice movement.

More like G8—Africa nil.

But it will not be enough. The failure of MPH to achieve its political demands cannot be laid at the door of Oxfam, Geldof and company alone. By being too dependent on corridor-lobbying, celebrities and the media, by failing to give voice and ownership of the campaign to Southern social movements, by watering down the radical demands agreed upon by hundreds of grassroots movements, from both the South and North, at the World Social Forum, and by politically legitimising the G8 summit, the campaign was doomed from the start.

Ten out of ten on aid, eight out of ten on debt? More like G8—Africa nil.

8

Celebrities Contribute to Philanthropy

Alexandra Marks

Alexandra Marks is a staff writer for the Christian Science Monitor.

Philanthropy is gaining new momentum, thanks in part to the efforts and influence of celebrity philanthropists. "Hyper-agents" of philanthropy, who include former president Bill Clinton, U2 lead singer Bono, and Microsoft head Bill Gates, use great sums of their own wealth to directly contribute to their causes and motivate others to do the same by acting as philanthropic role models and using the power and charisma that comes with celebrity status. These hyper-agents bring people together as never before—from many different social and political backgrounds— pushing philanthropy to new levels of practice and participation.

Call it the dawn of the Golden Age of Philanthropy. And one early manifestation was on display [in September 2005] at an elegant hotel in Midtown Manhattan. Kings, prime ministers, international entrepreneurs, media moguls, and savvy local business people met at the first annual Clinton Global Initiative to pledge themselves to take on a lofty set of once seemingly intransigent challenges: from international poverty and AIDS to global warming to ethnic and religious strife.

Alexandra Marks, "Celebrity 'Hyper-Agents' Transform Philanthropy," *Christian Science Monitor*, September 19, 2005. Reproduced by permission from Christian Science Monitor, www.csmonitor.com.

The goals were chosen because "together, they will determine in large measure the future of people all across the globe," said former President Bill Clinton at the opening session last Thursday.

This initiative, along with others, like the ONE Campaign, headlined by Microsoft's Bill Gates and U2 rock star Bono, and the Africa Initiative, started by British Prime Minister Tony Blair, are part of a philanthropic shift. Scholars like Paul Schervish call these the "fruits of dramatic change" in the nature and expression of people's natural tendency to reach out to help one another.

It's a result of a combination of factors that are emerging together for first time in history: One is that crises—from hurricane Katrina to the tsunami in the Indian Ocean to famine in Sudan—get delivered "right to our hearts through the media," says Professor Schervish. Combine this with the fact many Americans have the economic resources to help, and that makes it possible to "dream and to act."

[Hyper-agents] are celebrities with the wealth and time to dedicate to finding new ways of addressing age-old problems, as well as the charisma to motivate others.

"What we have are the first roots of a dramatic change in philanthropy that we're going to see emerge and become a regular part of our culture in the next 10 years," says Schervish, the director of the Boston College Center on Wealth and Philanthropy. "It's philanthropy as a natural dimension of people's economic and work life; it's becoming more regularly a category of expenditure even for those who aren't wealthy."

It's being spurred in part by individuals like Clinton, Bono, and Gates—people Schervish refers to as "hyper-agents." They are celebrities with the wealth and time to dedicate to finding new ways of addressing age-old problems, as well as the charisma to motivate others. At the weekend conference, Clinton said he was delighted to be able to bring together "so many people from seemingly divergent, even oppositional viewpoints in the same room.

"But I believe there is more that unites us than separates us and the issues we're going to discuss are too big for government or business or Republicans or Democrats or any single religious group to solve alone," he told the assembled crowd. "We've all come here today with a common purpose: to find real solutions—and to commit to do our part on four issues that plague modern society."

US Benefits from Can-do Tradition

Such individualistic, can-do tendencies have been part of the American culture since its inception.

As [French Political thinker] Alexis de Tocqueville noted in the early 1830s, the inclination for individuals to band together for the larger social good thrived in the nascent country because America lacked the aristocracy and formal church hierarchy that dealt with such social needs in Europe.

From firehouses to prisons to hospitals, local neighbors pooled their resources to create such institutions. In more recent generations, foundations and nongovernmental and church organizations took on the main philanthropic role. But now, as the nation matures in an age of globalization and Americans have more resources, that individualistic spirit is again asserting itself, producing a new kind of philanthropy.

Over the weekend, the Sheraton Hotel and Towers was packed with living examples: people such as Dr. Bruce Charash, a prominent New York cardiologist who started his own foundation called Apple P.I.E. It "translates science into English" so middle-school teachers can better understand what they're teaching. He came because of "the sense of optimism here."

And it's not just manifest in the spirit and ideas. Clinton, in his role as "hyper agent," has required that each participant make a pledge to address one problem over the next year. If they fail, they won't be invited back next year.

Dr. Charash's pledge: to create a new foundation called "Doc to Dock," which will allow the American medical community to donate extra resources directly to colleagues in developing nations, as well as set up an internet forum for collegial advice.

"We can get cardiologists to donate stethoscopes one year—10,000 or 20,000 of them—the next year we can get orthopedic surgeons to donate plaster and splinting materials," he says. "Clearly, there's been a great suspicion when donating to other nations, particularly, as to how much goes to the needy. This conference can find a better way to give direct access because there are some structural problems with [current] fundraising mechanisms."

The commitments made here were as diverse as the almost 1,000 participants from around the world. Some involved tens of millions of dollars, like the decision of the former head of Cel-Tel Africa, Mehamed Ibrahim, to give $100 million of his own to create the African Enterprise Private Investment Fund that will help nurture small- and medium-size businesses in Africa. Other pledges were more personal but no less compelling.

Vision for an 'Adopt a Family' Program

Retired United Nations staffer Muriel Glasgow, who now owns a public relations and marketing firm, wants to create an "adopt a family" program.

"Many agencies help individual children, but children come with a group, they have family, and there are many families in poverty in developing countries," says Ms. Glasgow. "When you put people-to-people with people-for-people, things change."

That sense of confidence and determination to make the world a better place was on display all weekend. For many it was a refreshing renewal, as well as a reminder of how much work needs to be done.

"On the one side, the stakes have never been higher, but on the other, very positive side, the possibilities have never been greater," says José Maria Figueres, the former president of Costa Rica. "To see so many different people coming together in a much more action-driven agenda is a terrific way to do things."

9

Celebrities Use Philanthropy for Financial and Personal Gain

Kimberly Elworthy

Kimberly Elworthy is a columnist for the Cord Weekly, *the official newspaper of Wilfred Laurier University in Waterloo, Canada.*

Celebrities endorse charities and participate in philanthropy with two goals in mind: profit and image. It can be called "capitalactivism"—celebs lend their names and starpower to market charitable products for profit and improve their public image. For instance, Africa has emerged as the biggest charity fad for celebrities, as they are guaranteed little to no press if they decide to undertake a domestic, little-known cause. In addition, it is companies—not charities—that decide how much money from the proceeds of charitable products, such as goods marketed under the (Product) Red Campaign, is actually donated to fight poverty, AIDS, and other global problems celebrities choose to "authenticate."

One recent afternoon I found myself in the metropolis of Canadian society—The Eaton Centre. Browsing through Sears, a very fit, hairless and not to mention topless male model informed me of a promotion: if I buy a new designer perfume today, part of the profit will go "to help Africa."

Considering Africa has about 61 countries, I felt obligated to ask what part of Africa they were trying to help and for

Kimberly Elworthy, "The Value of Celebrity Activism," *Cord Weekly*, October 24, 2007. Reproduced by permission.

what cause? Unsurprisingly, he did not have a clue and directed me to the main desk. The sales associates were similarly unaware of where my money would be going.

It is experiences such as this one that make me skeptical about people who choose to make "charity work" a commercial endeavour. When someone chooses to gain profit from other people's suffering and misfortune, it is simply unethical.

In the past couple of years, celebrity charity work has exploded. Paris Hilton is heading to Rwanda soon and Lindsay Lohan is shipping out to Kenya. Celebrities, products themselves, are using charity work to sell themselves and appeal to a "new and aware" youth market.

But what does it mean when a celebrity, who is usually more reckless, self-centered and indulgent than the average Joe, tries to tell us to open our eyes and give our well-earned money away to help those in need?

Cynics often say, according to *The New York Times*, that celebrity philanthropy is just a current fad and a way to get people, like Miss Lohan, a little good press after a rough year. Not only is charity a fad but Africa is the biggest thing out there this season. Africa is a continent torn by so many issues—poverty, AIDS, starvation, and genocide (in Darfur)—that everyone can help their cause of choice there.

Celebrity philanthropy has become Capitalactivism, which is when celebrities use their name and qualifications to authenticate charitable products.

It wouldn't make sense, of course, to help your own country first; the USA also is ripe with poverty, illiteracy and a non-existent public health care system. Helping your own country is not "in style," Adopting a local Caucasian baby doesn't scream out "I care."

Capitalactivism

The *Times* also goes on to say that celebrity philanthropy has become Capitalactivism, which is when celebrities use their name and qualifications to authenticate charitable products. An example of such capitalactivism is Bono's (Product) RED campaign, where the proceeds from red products will go to AIDS treatment and prevention.

It should be noted that all this money is not going to any research about AIDS, something that could actually stop AIDS forever. It is only going to things that suppress the effects of AIDS. It is also interesting that each company decides how much of the proceeds from each item will be donated to the campaign.

According to the (Product) RED website, American Express will donate one percent of your spending to the campaign and Motorola will give $8.50 (US) for each purchase of their red Razr cell-phone.

Apple doesn't even say how much they are willing to donate for each one gigabyte iPod shuttle.

Although it's better than nothing, we should not reduce a company's or a celebrity's interest in activism to nothing. It is the job of people who are bestowed with excesses of money to do good things with it. And this is because we all think that, "if I found myself in a situation where I needed help, someone would help me."

I don't see celebrities helping students get to places around the world where people need help. Students are now, and have always been, the future of society. These are the people who can truly dedicate their lives to a cause and who are looking for something to become passionate about.

They are also the people who can work towards a real solution through research instead of offering band-aids as Bono's (Product) Red campaign does.

This option, though, does not give celebrities and companies the necessary press coverage to make their good work pay off and so it will be neglected.

Celebrities neglect to assist students, who could actually make a difference in society, because they are more interested in promoting themselves through good press coverage than finding possible solutions to the issues people face around the world.

At the end of the day, celebrity activism is not about making change for the better. It is about profit. Right now, poverty, AIDS and war are prime marketing tools with which profit can be made.

10

Celebrities Can Be Role Models for Women

Aliza Pilar Sherman

Aliza Pilar Sherman is a writer and author and speaker on women's issues.

Famous, highly successful, ambitious women such as media mogul Oprah Winfrey, groundbreaking pop icon Madonna, and fashion designer Cynthia Rowley provide strong role models for women—especially when it comes to business. Such celebrities inspire other women to break out of the roles and stereotypes that can hold them back in the business world, where women often lack positive reinforcement. Rowley, whose expanding fashion-based business includes housewares and book publishing, is a prime role model for women who aspire to start their own companies. She and other famous women entrepreneurs show how women can be successful and distinctly female in the male-dominated world of business.

Oprah Winfrey has an entertainment empire. So does Madonna. Jennifer Lopez has added clothing and perfume to her numerous ventures. As celebrities continue to branch out into new lines of business, what lessons can noncelebrity business owners learn from them?

"I've learned many things from observing Oprah," says Alison Glander, 42, president and CEO of PowerPact LLC, a marketing agency in Midlothian, Virginia, with revenues of $17 million. "She puts herself out there, and people respond."

Aliza Pilar Sherman, "Star Qualities: How Celebrity Role Models Have Inspired Us," *Entrepreneur*, May 2004. Reproduced by permission.

Glander says typical management wisdom encourages company leaders to be stoic, invincible and untouchable; but Oprah has taught her you can let people in, and they'll pull for you. "The bonds between people in [your] company grow even stronger and more personal. And that's a proven way to reduce turnover—when people feel connected, like a family."

Another lesson Glander has learned from Oprah is not to be afraid to promote yourself. "It's a female thing—a temptation to hide in the shadows and thrust others into the spotlight," she admits, but Glander has realized a business needs its CEO to be "famous." Promotions that show a company has a strong leader attract more customers, says Glander.

For Sara Blakely, founder of Spanx Inc., a $12 million high-end hosiery, legwear and apparel company in Atlanta, Madonna has been a role model for years. "Seeing Madonna's courage in herself gave me a lot of strength," says Blakely, 32. When facing challenges starting her business, Blakely looked for inspiration. "I remembered reading stories about Madonna believing in herself when no one else did. I believed in my idea [for footless pantyhose] and knew it was up to me to make my product a reality."

In Blakely's opinion, Madonna is a marketing genius. "Part of her genius is doing things that are risky or edgy. When I decided to name my product 'Spanx,' I took a big gulp and thought 'Am I really going to try to sell a product with this name to a high-end, ultraconservative retail space like Neiman Marcus?" She decided to take a marketing risk, with positive results.

Relying on gut instinct is another trait Blakely sees in the Material Girl. "I believe Madonna trusts her gut in her decisions," says Blakely. "I've had no formal business classes or training, but I launched this business, built the brand, expanded my line and hired an amazing team. When I have to make a big decision, I rely on my team. But in the end, it's a serious gut check—and I don't let anyone mess with that."

While some celebrities become entrepreneurs, there are also entrepreneurs who become celebrities by virtue of their public images—like designer Cynthia Rowley, who has expanded from fashion into housewares, books and more. That made Rowley a perfect role model for Laura Eisman, 37, CEO and creative director of New York City-based Girlshop Inc., an online retailer of independent designer clothing for women, men and children that grossed $4 million in 2003. "I always loved Cynthia Rowley's designs," Eisman says. "Fashion is a competitive business, but Cynthia rose above the rest with offshoots of her brand, such as Swell, and smart partnerships [such as the one with] Target." As Eisman embarks on expanding the Girlshop brand into retail stores and TV, she says she's following Rowley's example.

Eisman sees Rowley's foray into writing as co-author of *Swell: A Girl's Guide to the Good Life* (Warner Books) as yet another creative way to extend her brand. And she gives high marks to Rowley's approach, which she summarizes as "being relatable. Everyone listens to the girl next door. Be familiar. Talk to your market, not at them. This gives you more power."

11

Celebrities Should Not Be Role Models for Women

Fiona Bawdon

Fiona Bawdon is a writer for New Statesman.

Celebrities are not good role models for women, particularly teenage girls. The fashion industry is known for its emphasis on a rail-thin body, and studies have shown that media images influence the self-esteem of adolescents. The number of teenage girls with eating disorders is increasing, and girls are getting eating disorders at younger ages than ever before. Many factors contribute to eating disorders, but media images are one thing that we can control, so we should do something to stop the onslaught of unhealthy images and role models we are presenting to our youth.

As London Fashion Week sashayed to a close on 20 September, most of the media coverage was of the clothes, rather than the skeletal frames of the girls inside them. Yet the week coincided with the publication of recommendations from a controversial inquiry into the health of fashion models, set up after two Latin American models died from eating disorders, one after collapsing on the catwalk.

Media Imagery Has a Direct Effect on Teenagers

In her report, the chair of the Model Health Inquiry, Baroness Kingsmill, said she had found "startling" evidence of the vulnerability of models, who are at "high risk" of eating disorders. The inquiry heard evidence from an editor who said she'd sat through "innumerable shows where I have been unable to take in the clothes through shock at the emaciated frames of models". A writer said the fashion world was "numb", looking at models only as "clothes hangers" and "failing to see whether they are healthy or not". The inquiry made 14 recommendations to improve the working lives of models, including banning under-16s from the catwalk and introducing compulsory medical checks and a trade union.

The importance of the report, however, is not just that it reveals exploitation of young women in the fashion industry. There is now a whole body of evidence that links fashion and media images directly to the health and well-being of the wider population of teenage girls.

Teenage girls say they are influenced by pictures of impossibly skinny women, even when they don't want to be.

In a study of 3,200 young women carried out in February this year by Girlguiding UK, over half of 16- to 25-year-olds said the media made them feel that "being pretty and thin" was the "most important thing". A quarter of girls aged between ten and 15 said the same. The most influential role models by far (cited by 95 per cent of girls) were Kate Moss and Victoria Beckham, both of whom are famously thin. In another study—*Sex, Drugs, Alcohol and Young People*, by the Independent Advisory Group on Sexual Health and HIV, published in June this year—nearly 30 per cent of 11-year-old girls expressed dissatisfaction with their body weight, and one in ten was on a diet. By age 15, 46 per cent of girls were unhappy with their weight, and a quarter of them were dieting.

Professionals working in this field are convinced that the number of teenage girls with an eating disorder is going up, and that sufferers are getting younger. The majority are aged 14–25, but girls as young as eight have been diagnosed. The last reliable survey into eating disorders across Britain dates back to 1990, but in Scotland, where new research was conducted in 2006, there had been a 40 per cent increase since 1990.

Teenage girls say they are influenced by pictures of impossibly skinny women, even when they don't want to be. At a recent conference in London about teenagers and the media, organised by the campaign group Women in Journalism, one teenager encapsulated the views of many of the 50 or so girls present, saying the fashion to be super-skinny made her "feel really ugly. I know it's really stupid but I still follow it. It makes me feel really insecure."

Adolescents Most at Risk

This young woman's experience is all too common, according to Professor Janet Treasure, director of the eating disorders unit at the the South London and Maudsley NHS Trust, who has conducted research into the impact of the "size zero culture". She says looking at pictures of thin women reduces self-esteem—and adolescents are among the most susceptible to these pressures. Adolescents are also the group most likely to suffer long-term ill-effects from eating disorders because their bodies are still developing.

Susan Ringwood, chief executive of beat, the eating disorders charity, gave evidence to the inquiry. She supports its conclusions, but says restricting its remit to protecting young women in the modelling industry, rather than tackling the impact of "size zero" culture on the wider population, was an opportunity missed.

Ringwood accepts that it's a gross oversimplification to blame the rise in eating disorders entirely on the media's focus on thinness and dieting, but says it does play a part. "Eating disorder sufferers say: 'How come its OK for celebrities to look like that and not me? How come they're being celebrated on the front of a magazine and I'm in hospital being told I'm going to die?'"

Although the Model Health Inquiry acknowledged this is an area outside its remit, it included a recommendation for a code of conduct to govern the digital manipulation of photos. The inquiry heard evidence of retouching to make models look thinner or even to make ill models look well—something of great concern to those working with eating disorder sufferers. "These processes add pressure to models to meet an unattainable ideal," it said. One suggestion was for retouched photos to carry a "health warning" so that the reader knows what she's looking at isn't real. The teenagers at the London conference were previously unaware that magazine images are routinely airbrushed: thighs slimmed, wrinkles smoothed and blemishes removed.

Of course, media coverage of skinny women is far from universally positive. But even critical coverage of celebrities who are deemed to be "too thin" can make matters worse for eating disorder sufferers, according to Ringwood. Low self-esteem is a recognised factor: sufferers don't think they are worthy of taking up any space in the world, and shrink accordingly. Seeing bodies that look similar to theirs being pilloried and described as revolting reinforces their own lack of self-worth, she says.

Bodies Beautiful

Ringwood acknowledges that the causes of eating disorders are many and complex; they include factors such as genetic disposition and personality type, often compounded by traumatic events—for instance, bereavement or bullying. "But the final piece of the jigsaw is the social context," she says. Add the media, which celebrate impossibly skinny bodies over all other types, and numbers of sufferers are bound to increase. She would welcome a move for magazines to specify when images have been retouched.

It is a view shared by many of the sufferers themselves. Asked what was the one thing that would help prevent such conditions, most sufferers said it would be for the media to show more "real" bodies. They ranked this as more important than greater understanding from parents, or even greater medical knowledge. "Why can't the media promote healthy, normal-sized people?" lamented one typical respondent.

Ringwood says the media and the fashion industry should present a more diverse mix of body types as beautiful and acceptable. Such a change would not be a total solution by any means, but it would help, she argues. "We can't change brain chemistry and we can't protect young women from all forms of trauma. Of all the factors involved in eating disorders, images in the media are the one area we can change."

- 4 is the UK dress size equivalent to the notorious US "size zero"

- 23 inches is the size of Victoria Beckham's waist

- 34 inches is the waist size of the average British woman

- 40% of teenage girls consider cosmetic surgery

- 1.15m estimated cases of eating disorders in the UK

- 92% of young people with an eating disorder can't talk about it

- 3 catwalk models have died after starvation diets in the past year

- 90% of those suffering from eating disorders are female

Organizations to Contact

The editors have compiled the following list of organizations concerned with the issues debated in this book. The descriptions are derived from materials provided by the organizations. All have publications or information available for interested readers. The list was compiled on the date of publication of the present volume; the information provided here may change. Be aware that many organizations take several weeks or longer to respond to inquiries, so allow as much time as possible.

Action Against Hunger/Action Contre la Faim (ACF)
U.S. Office, New York, NY   10018
Web site: www.actionagainsthunger.org

As part of the ACF International Network, Action Against Hunger is a relief organization dedicated to supplying emergency aid and providing long-term solutions to hunger, nutrition, sanitation, health care, and other humanitarian issues across the globe. ACF was established in France in 1979 and assists five million people in forty countries.

Amnesty International (AI)
1 Easton Street, London   WC 1X 0DW
  United Kingdom
+44-20-74135500 • fax: +44-20-79561157
Web site: www.amnesty.org

Founded in 1961, AI is a United Kingdom-based nongovernmental organization that seeks to protect basic human rights and the freedom of speech, ending the violation and abuses of these rights around the world. It has over 2.2 million members and subscribers in over 150 countries and regions.

AVERT
4 Brighton Road, Horsham, West Sussex   RH13 5BA
   United Kingdom
Web site: www.avert.org

AVERT is an international HIV and AIDS charity based in the United Kingdom. AVERT has HIV and AIDS projects in countries where there is a particularly high rate of infection, such as South Africa, or where there is a rapidly increasing rate of infection, such as in India. The organization brings AIDS education and information to people in almost every country in the world through its website.

Debt Aids Trade Africa (DATA)
1400 Eye Street, NW, Washington, DC   20005
(202) 639-8010
Web site: www.data.org

DATA is an advocacy organization dedicated to ending extreme poverty and AIDS in Africa. Founded by U2 lead singer Bono, Bobby Shriver, and activists from the Jubilee "Drop the Debt" campaign in 2002, DATA calls on the governments of the world's wealthiest nations to keep their existing commitments to Africa and adopt new trade and aid policies that will help Africans put themselves on the path to long-term prosperity and stability.

Global Call to Action Against Poverty (GCAP)
c/o CIVICUS, PO Box 933, Southdale, Johannesburg   2135
   South Africa
+ 27 11 833 59 59 • fax: + 27 11 833 97 79
email: info@whiteband.org
Web site: www.whiteband.org

Formed in 2004, GCAP is a growing alliance of trade unions, community groups, faith groups, women and youth organizations, nongovernmental organizations, and other campaigners working together across more than 100 national platforms to end poverty and promote civil rights.

Make Poverty History
c/o BOND, Regent's Wharf, 8 All Saint's Street
London   N1 9RL
   United Kingdom
Web site: www.makepovertyhistory.org

Make Poverty History is a campaign led by a coalition of British and Irish organizations, from charities to religious groups and other agencies. Its goal is to end extreme poverty and promote fair trade through increasing awareness and influencing government action.

Not On Our Watch
email: info@notonourwatchproject.org
Web site: www.notonourwatchproject.org

Not On Our Watch is a nonprofit agency that aims to focus global attention and resources towards putting an end to mass atrocities around the world. Drawing on the powerful voices of artists, activists and cultural leaders, including George Clooney, Brad Pitt, Don Cheadle, Matt Damon, Jerry Weintraub, David Pressman, Not On Our Watch generates lifesaving humanitarian assistance and protection for the vulnerable, marginalized, and displaced.

The ONE Campaign
1400 Eye Street, NW, Suite 601, Washington, DC   20005
(202) 552-4990
Web site: www.one.org

ONE is a campaign of over 2.4 million people from all 50 states and over 100 of America's nonprofit, advocacy, and humanitarian organizations. Its objective is to raise public awareness about issues of global poverty, hunger, disease, and efforts to fight such problems in the world's poorest countries.

People for the Ethical Treatment of Animals (PETA)
501 Front Street, Norfolk, VA   23510
(757) 622-PETA (7382) • fax: (757) 622-0457

Web site: www.peta.org

PETA, with more than 2 million members and supporters, is the largest animal rights organization in the world. PETA focuses its attention on the four areas in which the largest numbers of animals suffer the most intensely for the longest periods of time: on factory farms, in laboratories, in the clothing trade, and in the entertainment industry. The organization works through public education, cruelty investigations, research, animal rescue, legislation, special events, celebrity involvement, and protest campaigns.

Raising Malawi
1100 South Robertson Boulevard, Los Angeles, CA   90035
(310) 867-2881
Web site: www.raisingmalawi.org

Raising Malawi is a nongovernmental organization that provides humanitarian aid to the 1 million Malawian orphans living in extreme poverty. Co-founded by Madonna and Kabbalah Center co-director Michael Berg in 2006, Raising Malawi uses a community-based approach to provide immediate direct physical assistance, create long-term sustainability, support education and psychosocial programs, and build public awareness through multimedia and worldwide volunteer efforts.

The SOS (Save Our Selves) Campaign
email: info@liveearth.org
Web site: www.liveearth.org

Helmed by music producer Kevin Wall and former U.S. vice president and environmental activist Al Gore, the mission of the SOS campaign is to change consumer behaviors and motivate corporations and political leaders to enact decisive measures to combat the climate crisis. SOS promoted the Live Earth concert series held in July 2007, which was held in different parts of the world and included over 150 bands and artists.

United Nations (UN)
First Avenue at 46th Street, New York, NY   10017
(212) 963-8687
Web site: www.un.org

Founded in 1945 to replace the League of Nations, the UN is an international organization that includes 192 member states. Its aim is to protect human rights, enforce international laws, and promote social progress. Its agencies include the World Health Organization (WHO) and United Nations Children's Fund (UNICEF).

Bibliography

Books

Gëzim Alpion   *Mother Teresa: Saint or Celebrity?*
                    New York, NY: Routledge, 2006.

Ernest Cashmore   *Celebrity/Culture.* New York, NY:
                    Routledge, 2006.

Andrew F. Cooper   *Celebrity Diplomacy.* Boulder, CO:
                    Paradigm Publishers, 2008.

Susan J. Drucker   *Heroes in a Global World.* Cresskill,
and Gary   NJ: Hampton Press, 2008.
Gumpert, eds.

Jake Halpern   *Fame Junkies: The Hidden Truths Be-
                    hind America's Favorite Addiction.*
                    Boston, MA: Houghton Mifflin Com-
                    pany, 2007.

Daniel Herwitz   *The Star as Icon: Celebrity in the Age
                    of Mass Consumption.* New York, NY:
                    Columbia University Press, 2008.

Su Holmes and   *Framing Celebrity: New Directions in
Sean Redmond   Celebrity Culture.* New York, NY:
                    Routledge, 2006.

Barron H. Lerner   *When Illness Goes Public: Celebrity
                    Patients and How We Look at Medi-
                    cine.* Baltimore, MD: Johns Hopkins
                    University Press, 2006.

Mary-Lane Kamberg   *Bono: Fighting World Hunger and Poverty.* New York, NY: Rosen Publishing Group, 2007.

P. David Marshall   *The Celebrity Culture Reader.* New York, NY: Routledge, 2006.

Periodicals

Alan Cowell   "The Politics of Aid and Celebrities' Mass Activism," *International Herald-Tribune*, July 1, 2005.

Linda Diebel   "The Dark Side to Oprah's Big Give," *Toronto Star*, April 19, 2008.

Daniel W. Drezner   "Should Celebrities Set the World Agenda?" *Los Angeles Times*, December 30, 2007.

Adam Elkus   "Celebrity Colonialism: From Madonna to Kate Moss, Buying Africa Is the Latest Trend Among the Famous," *Colorlines*, March–April 2007.

Donna Freydkin   "Celebrity Activists Put Star Power to Good Use," *USAToday*, June 23, 2006.

Michael Fullilove   "Celebrities Should Stick to Their Day Jobs," *Financial Times*, February 1, 2006.

Rachel Giese   "Handle with Care: How Diana Invented Modern Day Celebrity Activism," CBC.ca, June 27, 2007.

Kate Bowman Johnston   "Celebrity Activists," *Sojourners*, July 2006.

Tom Junod   "Angelina Jolie Dies for Our Sins,"
                   Esquire, July 2007.

Andrew Mueller   "Rebels with a Cause," *Guardian*,
                   September 23, 2006.

Emily Nussbaum   "The Nuclear Family, Exploded," *New
                   York*, August 20, 2007.

Amrita Shah   "With Great Glamour, Great Respon-
                   sibility?" *Indian Express*, April 3,
                   2008.

Jean-Claude   "All Rock, No Action," *New York
Shanda Tomne   Times*, July 15, 2005.

Bryan Walsh   "What Live Earth Really Meant,"
                   Time, July 8, 2007.

Erin Wiley   "Celebrities Offer Poor Role Models,"
                   University Daily Kansan, January 20,
                   2006.

Index

L

Land mines, 46
Lange, Jessica, 29
Lennon, John, 8, 35
Lewis, Mike, 65
Live 8 concert series, 20–24, 28, 34, 46, 53–65
Live Aid, 35, 41, 46
Live Earth concert series, 41, 47, 48, 86
Lohan, Lindsay, 9, 16, 40, 72
Lopez, Jennifer, 75

M

MacArthur, Dame Ellen, 33
Madonna, 7, 9, 41, 45, 47, 75–76, 86
Madre (human rights organization), 59
Make Poverty History (MPH), 34, 53–56, 57–59, 61–65, 85
Malawi, 7
Malaysia, 61
Mandela, Nelson, 46, 48
Manji, Firoze, 64
Marks, Alexandra, 66–70
Martin, Chris, 27–28
McCain, John, 44
McCartney, Paul, 35
Melamed, Claire, 61
Milne, Kirsty, 54–56
Model Health Inquiry, 78, 81
Models, 78–82. *See also specific names*
Moore, Michael, 49
Moss, Kate, 79
Motorola, 73
MPH (Make Poverty History), 34, 53–56, 57–59, 61–65, 85

MTV, 44–45
Mutombo, Dikembe, 44

N

Naidoo, Kumi, 58, 63, 64
National Rifle Association (NRA), 21
Nestlé, 64
New Labour, 62, 65
New Statesman (periodical), 78
New York Times, 15, 48, 72, 73
Newsweek (magazine), 40
Nobel Peace Prize, 39, 41
Not On Our Watch, 85
Notting Hill (film), 53
NRA (National Rifle Association), 21

O

Obama, Barack, 8-9, 44
Ogrizek, Michel, 29–30
Olympics, 13, 47
One Campaign, 15–16, 20–24, 67, 85
Orth, Maureen, 14
Ottawa Convention, 46
Oxfam, 62–65

P

Pakistan, 31
Paltrow, Gwyneth, 28
Peace Corps, 15
Penn, Sean, 27, 48
People for the Ethical Treatment of Animals (PETA), 85–86
People (magazine), 18, 25
Peoples' Gold Association, 33
Perez Hilton, 18
"Philanthropic advisors" for celebrities, 43